Odd Dates Only

Odd Dates Only

The Bizarre Birthday Book

William Hartston

SOUVENIR PRESS

First published 1998 by Souvenir Press Ltd,
43 Great Russell Street, London WC1B 3PA

ISBN 0 285 63466 6

Typeset by Rowland Phototypesetting Ltd,
Bury St Edmunds, Suffolk.
Printed in Great Britain by
Creative Print and Design Group (Wales), Ebbw Vale

'Manna and dates, in argosy transferr'd
From Fez; and spiced dainties, every one'

John Keats, *The Eve of St Agnes*

Preface

There is no shortage of books about anniversaries. If you want to know when the kings and queens of Europe and their prime ministers were born and died, when their wars began and ended and when they signed peace treaties with other nations, you will find them with ease. If you simply want a list of saints' feast days, with no explanation of who those saints were or, indeed, any indication of whether they existed at all, you will find it in such books or in any dull national newspaper.

But where will you find the precise date on which a woman first made a bungee-jump from a paraglider? This book is a compilation of the anniversaries that other compilers have overlooked or chosen to ignore. Among the profusion of historical dates, these are surely what Keats was referring to when he wrote of 'spiced dainties'.

I am grateful to those who have trodden the date-collectors' path before me, whose works I have scavenged for oddities. Among those I have found useful I must mention particularly *The Pan Book of Dates* (1990), *A Dictionary of Dates* (Oxford University Press, 1993) and *On This Day* (Hamlyn, 1992), all of which have yielded several gems nestling among worthy anniversary items. The Internet, too, offers a wide range of anniversary sites of varying usefulness and interest. For an electronic plethora of dates of all kinds, I can particularly recommend Scope Systems' site (www.scopesys.com). I have also trawled newspapers and news wires, dictionaries of saints and a wide range of encyclopaedias, ancient and modern, for the material that appears in these pages.

I am particularly grateful to Sue Phillpott for her meticulous checking of my manuscript, despite my inclusion of so much inherently uncheckable material, and her many suggestions for improving this work. Any errors that remain in these pages, however, are entirely the responsibility of the author.

At the very least, I hope this book will provide the motorist who encounters a sign saying 'Parking on this side of the road on odd dates only' with ample evidence that there is not a single date in the year that isn't very odd indeed.

William Hartston, London
St Oliver Plunkett's Day, 1998

1 January
Feast day of St Almachius

Good day to: *start a diary*
Favourite drink: *pale ale*
Favourite meal: *lunch*

St Almachius was killed around AD 400, when he rushed into a Roman arena and tried to stop the gladiators fighting.

New Year's Day has been celebrated on this date since the British Calendar Act of 1752. Before that, the year officially began on 25 March. Julius Caesar introduced the Julian Calendar on 1 January 46 BC. Samuel Pepys chose 1 January 1660 to start his *Diary*.

1 January is a natural date to start new enterprises and end old ones: in 1808, the import of slaves to the USA was ended; in 1913, the US parcel post service was introduced; in 1876 the first British trademark was registered—to Bass Pale Ale; this was the day in 1890 when football nets were first used in goal; in 1955 luncheon vouchers went on sale in Britain; and in 1961 the farthing ceased to be legal tender.

Notable births: J. Edgar Hoover of the FBI (1895), Kim Philby of the KGB (1912).

---

2 January

Lucky language: *French*
Unlucky language: *Latin*
Happy ending: *cremation*

This was the date in 1987 when Macdonald publishers succumbed to political correctness and announced that golliwogs would no longer appear in Enid Blyton's *Noddy* books, but would be replaced by gnomes. Though a good day for gnomes, this is a bad day for midgets, being the date in 1883 when Charles Stratton alias General Tom Thumb died. He was 79 centimetres (31 inches) tall.

The Latin language suffered a double blow on this day in AD 17 with the deaths of the poet Ovid and the historian Livy. The French language, however, had a good day in 1635, when Cardinal Richelieu established the Académie Française, in order to maintain its purity.

In 1900, this was a good day to travel in New York, as the first electric omnibus service began, and a good day to die in Hull, where Britain's first municipal crematorium opened for business.

Quote of the day: 'We are not amused'—written by Queen Victoria on this date in 1900.

3 January

Favourite pastime: *drinking through straws*
Lucky vocation: *Pope*
Lucky direction: *south*

3 January is, above all, a good day for excommunications. Pope Leo X excommunicated Martin Luther on this date in 1521, while in 1962 Pope John XXIII did the same to Fidel Castro. With the schisms implied by such actions, it will be no surprise to learn that this was the day in 1918 that Ernest Rutherford announced the splitting of the atom. To counterbalance all this, a large measure of unity was re-established when Alaska became the 49th state of the USA in 1959, supplanting Texas as the largest state.

This is a good day for travel, with Sir Edmund Hillary reaching the South Pole in 1958, and Oscar Wilde arriving in New York in 1882 when he told customs officers, 'I have nothing to declare except my genius.' Either of these events could be celebrated by drinking champagne through a straw, to commemorate the patenting of paper drinking-straws by Marvin C. Stone on 3 January 1888.

Notable births: Cicero (106 BC), J. R. R. Tolkien (1892).

4 January

Lucky part of the body: *appendix*
Unlucky bodily accessory: *moustache*
Bad day for: *Nobel Prize winners for Literature*

This is a good day for coincidences. It was the birthday in 1914 of both Jane Wyman (who married Ronald Reagan) and her daughter Maureen in 1941. It was also the date of the deaths of two men who won the Nobel Prize for Literature: Albert Camus, killed in a car crash at the age of 46 in 1960, and T. S. Eliot, who died in 1965 at the age of 76.

While writers may thus grieve on this date, barbers can hardly be much happier, for it was the date in 1961 when the apprentice barbers in Copenhagen finally gave up their strike which had begun in 1938 — the longest strike in history.

Dr William W. Grant performed the first successful appendectomy on this date in 1885, in Iowa, on a 22-year-old farmworker named Mary Gartside.

Notable death: in 1988, Karni Bheel, whose 7ft 10in (2.4m) moustache was the longest in India, was found decapitated. He is believed to have been murdered by rivals for the longest-moustache title.

5 January

Unlucky profession: *ticket collector*
Unlucky accessory: *hat*
Bad day for: *the world*

On 5 January 1797 John Hetherington, inventor of the top-hat, was charged before the Lord Mayor of London with having 'appeared on a public highway wearing upon his head a tall structure having a shining lustre and calculated to frighten timid people'. He was bound over to keep the peace, with a £50 fine if he reoffended.

Other notable events on this day were the opening in 1964, at Stamford Brook station, of the first automatic ticket barrier on the London Underground, and the founding of the Nazi Party by Adolf Hitler in 1919.

This is the birthday of two kings: Juan Carlos of Spain (1938) and King Camp Gillette, the razor-blade pioneer (1855). It was also the day in 1066 when Edward the Confessor died.

Quote of the day: 'How could they tell?'—Dorothy Parker on 5 January 1933 when informed that President Calvin Coolidge had died.

6 January

Twelfth Night

Favourite colours: *first blue, then red*
Good day for: *marrying a president*
Lucky number: *452*

This was the day of birth, in 1745, of Jacques-Étienne Montgolfier, the younger of the brothers who made the first successful flight in a hot-air balloon. It was probably just a coincidence, however, that the German airline Lufthansa was founded on the same day in 1926, and that on 6 January 1969 Jimmy Carter saw a UFO. He described it as 'bluish at first, then reddish, but not solid'.

On 6 January 1759, George Washington married Martha Custis; and on 6 January 1945, George Bush married Barbara Pierce.

This was the birthday in 1943 of English football manager Terry Venables and in 1959 of Indian cricket captain Kapil Dev. Of greater sporting significance, however, Don Bradman played his first innings for New South Wales on this day in 1930 and scored 452 runs.

Quote of the day: 'You have sent me a Flanders mare'—King Henry VIII on seeing Anne of Cleves, on their wedding day in 1540.

7 January

Favourite mode of transport: *balloon*
Auspicious planet: *Jupiter*
Unlucky acronym: *CQD*

This was the date of the first balloon crossing of the English Channel, by Jean-Pierre Blanchard and John Jeffries of Boston, Massachusetts, in 1785. With great foresight, Blanchard also invented the parachute.

Anyone ballooning to Pisa on this day in 1990 would have been disappointed to hear that the Leaning Tower had just been ruled unsafe and closed to the public for the first time in 807 years. Anyone visiting the planet Jupiter, however, could celebrate the anniversary of the discovery by Galileo in 1610 of its four moons.

This was the day in 1904 when the international distress signal CQD (CQ for 'seek you' and D for 'danger') was adopted. It lasted only two years before being replaced by SOS.

Notable events of 7 January 1927 include the opening of the first transatlantic telephone service between New York and London and the founding of the Harlem Globetrotters by Abraham Saperstein of Chicago.

8 January

Favourite food: *soup*
Unlucky food: *bacon sandwiches*
Bad day for: *flirting*

On 8 January 1880, the first soup kitchens for the poor were opened in London. (By pure coincidence it was also the date of the birth in 1926 of an American comedian known as Soupy Sales.) The authorities were to cut back on food, though, on the same day in 1940, when butter, bacon and sugar were rationed.

Elvis Presley was born on this day in 1935, and celebrated his 38th birthday in 1973 by suing his wife, Priscilla, for divorce. The date was never a good one for romance, since it was the day in 1902 when New York outlawed flirting in public.

Musical births: Shirley Bassey (1937) and David Bowie (1947).

While clearly good for singing, the date breaks even for physics, with the death of Galileo in 1642 and the birth of Stephen Hawking exactly 300 years later. It was also the birthday of suspense novelists Dennis Wheatley (1897) and Wilkie Collins (1824), whose *Woman in White* has been hailed as the first real detective story.

9 January

Auspicious profession: *tax collector*
Unlucky number: *63*
Bad day for: *having sex in a helicopter*

Unpopular events of the day: (1) the introduction of income tax in Britain by William Pitt the Younger in 1799, levied at a rate of two shillings in the pound (10 per cent) to help finance the war against France; (2) the birth of Richard Nixon in 1913.

Others with this birthday were more entertaining: Gracie Fields (1898), Susannah York and Joan Baez (both 1941), and the lady who turned strip-tease into an art form, Gypsy Rose Lee (1914).

X-rated anniversaries: 1951, when the first British 'X' certificate was awarded to the film *La Vie Commence Demain*; 1989, when a hotel in Tiberias, Israel, lost its kosher food licence for allowing a couple to have sex in a helicopter above its swimming-pool.

In 1980, Saudi Arabia beheaded 63 people for their involvement in a raid on the Grand Mosque in Mecca. The victims were eight years too early to benefit from the low-cost plastic tombstone, patented by Edgar Dakin of Yorkshire on this day in 1988.

10 January

Favourite drink: *tea*
Unlucky animal: *pig*
Bad day for: *trying out a new car*

In 1457 on this date, a sow was convicted of infanticide at Savigny in France and sentenced to death; later, six piglets were arrested for complicity. French-speakers' love of animals was evidently slow to recover, since it was not until 10 January 1929 that we saw the first adventures of Tintin and his dog Snowy as drawn by Hergé.

Despite the fact that this day saw the maiden flight of the first flying boat in New York in 1912, and the first Underground railway (from Paddington to Farringdon Street) in London in 1863, Sir Clive Sinclair still chose 10 January 1985 for the first demonstration of his ill-fated C5 electric car. A more successful launch happened in 1839 with the first auction of Indian tea in London.

Other innovations of the day include the penny post, launched by Sir Rowland Hill in 1840, and the 45 rpm extended-play gramophone record, launched by RCA in 1949; and on 10 January 1868, 451 convicts arrived in Australia, the last ever to be deported there.

11 January

Favourite drink: *milk*
Favourite food: *rhubarb*
Lucky disease: *diabetes*

In 1770 on this day, Benjamin Franklin sent a consignment of rhubarb from London to his friend John Bartram in Philadelphia—the first shipment of rhubarb to the United States.

The first state lottery was drawn on this date in 1569 at St Paul's Cathedral, London. Tickets were available at the cathedral, despite opposition from critics who said it encouraged crime.

This has been a terrible date for smokers: in 1964, the US surgeon-general issued a report saying for the first time that smoking might damage your health. That was 18 years to the day too late for King Zog of Albania, who was famed for smoking more than 100 cigarettes a day and who was deposed on this day in 1946.

11 January 1878 was the first time milk was delivered in glass bottles rather than being ladled from a churn into customers' own containers, and on 11 January 1922, in Toronto, Leonard Thompson became the first person successfully treated for diabetes with insulin.

12 January

Auspicious animal: *giant panda*
Unlucky life-form: *insects*
Unlucky subject: *mathematics*

This was the date of birth, in 1577, of Jean-Baptiste van Helmont, the Belgian chemist who invented the word 'gas' (from the Greek *khaos*, chaos). It was also the birthday, in 1899, of Paul Hermann Müller, the Swiss biochemist who formulated the insecticide DDT, for which he won the Nobel Prize in 1948. Millions of dead insects later, this same date in 1988 brought some good news for the animal kingdom, with the announcement in China that it is possible to breed test-tube giant pandas using frozen panda sperm.

Other notable births on this date include the Nazi leader Hermann Goering (1893) and the South African president P. W. Botha (1916).

Agatha Christie died on this date in 1976—exactly 28 years to the day after the opening of the first supermarket in Britain at Manor Park, London. This was also the date, in 1665, of the death of the great French mathematician Pierre de Fermat, whose 'last theorem' took another 330 years to solve.

13 January

Favourite sport: *frisbee-throwing*
Bad day for: *music*
Good day for: *a riot*

Scarcely any day in history has had such an effect on our leisure activities. On 13 January 1854, Anthony Faas of Philadelphia ruined for many the enjoyment of music by patenting the accordion. On 13 January 1906, the first advertisement for a radio receiver appeared in *Scientific American*; the 'Telimco' sold for $7.50 and had a range of one mile. Most significant change of all, however: on 13 January 1957 the Wham-O company developed the first frisbee.

This date is also notable for the worst sporting riot in history, at the Roman games in Constantinople in 532. Fighting spilled out on to the streets, and the resulting battles left an estimated 30,000 dead. This was also the day in 1979 when the Young Men's Christian Association filed a libel suit, later dropped, against the group Village People for their single 'YMCA'.

Notable deaths: Wyatt Earp, peacefully in bed at the age of 80 in 1929; James Joyce in 1941.

14 January

Favourite film: Casablanca
Favourite book: Alice in Wonderland
Most favoured disease: *leprosy*

On this day one man was born and one died, whose names became household words. 1741 saw the birth of Benedict Arnold, synonym for treachery after he deserted from the American army and defected to the British. In 1742, the comet-spotter Esmond Halley died.

Other notable births and deaths include Albert Schweitzer (born 14 January 1875), who won the Nobel Peace Prize in 1952 for his work against leprosy and sleeping sickness in French Equatorial Africa; the Reverend Charles Lutwidge Dodgson (died on this day in 1898), theologian and maths lecturer, better known as Lewis Carroll; and Humphrey Bogart (died 14 January 1957), who starred in such great films as *Casablanca*, *The Maltese Falcon* and *The African Queen*, the last of which won him an Oscar.

Quote of the day: 'Believe me, Saturdays will never seem the same. I'll miss you' —Ronald Reagan in his 331st and last weekly radio address to the nation in 1989.

15 January

Adults' Day in Japan

Propitious sport: *basketball*
Unlucky sport: *ice-skating*
Lucky profession: *mutineer*

This was the day in 1558 when Elizabeth I became Queen of England. It is generally not a bad day for heads of state, since it was also the date in 1919 when the pianist Ignace Jan Paderewski became the first premier of Poland, and also the date of the birth in 1918 of Gamal Nasser, who became premier of Egypt.

On this day in 1790 Fletcher Christian and his fellow mutineers on the *Bounty* landed on Pitcairn Island, where they and their descendants were unable to play basketball for 102 years, since the rules of the game were not published until 15 January 1892, when they appeared for the first time in *Triangle* magazine.

The greatest recorded disaster on this date occurred in 1867 when the ice gave way on the frozen lake in London's Regent's Park, and 40 people who had been skating and playing on it were killed.

Notable death: Nelson's mistress, Emma Hamilton (1815).

16 January

Bad day to: *go to the theatre*
Even worse day to: *go out for a drink*
Appropriate adjective: *'terrible'*

A 30-year-old tradition ended on this date in 1985, when publisher Hugh Hefner announced that *Playboy* magazine would no longer be held together with staples, thus sparing its models a painful-looking indignity. The legal sale of alcoholic beverages in the United States also ended on this day, when prohibition came into force in 1920.

On 16 January 1769, a riot occurred at the Haymarket Theatre, London, caused by members of the audience who had bought tickets to see a conjuror who failed to turn up—he had promised to get into a quart bottle and sing some songs.

Other notable events: Ivan the Terrible became the first tsar of Russia in 1547, and in 1991 Operation Desert Storm began to drive Iraqi forces out of Kuwait.

Understatement of the day: 'We're grateful for the offer'—Ronald Reagan, in 1986, on receiving Mikhail Gorbachev's proposal to rid the world of nuclear weapons by the year 2000.

17 January

Feast day of St Anthony, patron saint of pigs

Recommended profession: *boxer*
Favourite room: *lavatory*
Beware of: *earthquakes*

Two world heavyweight boxing champions were born on this day: Muhammad Ali (born Cassius Marcellus Clay in 1942) and Joe Frazier (1944). It was also the birthday in 1706 of Benjamin Franklin.

Disasters of the day: in 1994 an earthquake killed 61 in California; in 1995, an earthquake killed over 6,000 in Kobe, Japan.

On 17 January 1773, Captain Cook's ship *Resolution* became the first to cross the Antarctic Circle; 139 years later Robert Falcon Scott reached the South Pole, on 17 January 1912—just a month after Amundsen had beaten him to it.

Notable deaths: Thomas Crapper (1910), pioneer of the flush lavatory; and Chang and Eng Bunker (1874), the most famous Siamese twins. Never separated, they lived to the age of 63 and fathered 21 children.

Notable births: James Madison Randolph (1806), grandson of Thomas Jefferson and the first child to be born in the White House.

18 January

Vocational calling: *children's author*
Favourite food: *sandwich*
Inevitable type of bread: *unsliced*

Three noted children's authors were born on this day: A. A. Milne (1882), best known for *Winnie-the-Pooh*; Arthur Ransome (1884), remembered mainly for *Swallows and Amazons*; and Raymond Briggs (1934), who came to fame with *Fungus the Bogeyman* and *Father Christmas*. Hans Christian Andersen was neither born nor died on this date, but Danny Kaye, who played him in the film biography, was born on 18 January 1913.

On 18 January 1778, James Cook discovered the islands now known as Hawaii, which he named the Sandwich Islands, after the same Earl of Sandwich who gave his name to a type of fast food.

Sandwiches in the USA were affected by a wartime ban on sliced bread which came into force on 18 January 1943 in an attempt to reduce demand for metal replacement parts in bread-slicing machines. This was also the date in 1909 when brewers in New Zealand decided to abolish barmaids.

19 January

Good day for: *being hanged*
Bad day for: *being beheaded*
Lucky continent: *Antarctica*

On this day in 1728, Margaret Dickson opened her coffin and climbed out of it after she had been hanged for infanticide. Her innocence was later established. No such reprieve was available to Louis XVI of France who was guillotined in 1793, nor for Henry Howard, Earl of Surrey, courtier, poet and soldier, who was beheaded for high treason in 1547.

The author Julian Barnes and the singer Dolly Parton were both born on 19 January 1946, thus sharing a birthday with Edgar Allan Poe (1809). In 1840 on this date, Antarctica was discovered by Charles Wilkes and in 1903 a new bicycle race was instigated in Paris: it would be called the Tour de France.

The most pungent event on this date was the opening of Carl Andre's exhibit 'American Decay' at the Preteth Gallery, Washington, in 1973, which contained 227 kilos (500 lb) of cottage cheese and 45 litres (10 gal) of tomato ketchup. It was closed the next day because of the smell.

20 January

St Agnes Eve

Good day for: *virgins*
Bad day for: *actresses*
Mixed day for: *the Channel Tunnel*

This is St Agnes Eve when, according to Keats' poem, 'young virgins might have visions of delight'. Old actresses have done less well: Barbara Stanwyck died in 1990 and Audrey Hepburn in 1993.

An even more notable death on this day in 1936 was that of King George V, whose last words were, according to differing reports, either 'How is the Empire?' or 'Bugger Bognor.' His death led to King Edward VIII becoming, on that day, the first English king to fly in an aeroplane.

On 20 January 1975, England and France abandoned a proposal to go ahead with the Channel Tunnel; on 20 January 1986, England and France decided to go ahead with the proposal for a Channel Tunnel. On 20 January 1952, Patricia McCormick of Big Spring, Texas, made her debut in Mexico as the first professional female bullfighter.

21 January
Nuestra Señora de Altagracia Day in the Dominican Republic

Good day for: *nudity*
Bad day for: *smoking in public*
Lucky fruit: *pineapple*

In 1908 on this day, Katie Mulcahey was the first person to be arrested in New York under a new law that banned women from smoking in public.

In 1677 America's first medical publication appeared—a pamphlet on smallpox. Exactly 122 years later, on 21 January 1799, Edward Jenner introduced smallpox vaccination.

Notable events: on this day in 1813 the pineapple was introduced to Hawaii; in 1853 Russell Hawes patented an envelope-folding machine; in 1942 a magistrate in the Bronx ruled pinball machines illegal; in 1986 the Nude Olympics were held in Indiana, outdoors in a temperature of 3°C (37°F); in 1990 John McEnroe became the first tennis-player to be expelled from the Australian Open for swearing at an official.

Notable birthday coincidence: 1924, Benny Hill and Telly Savalas.

Notable deaths: Vladimir Lenin (1924), George Orwell (1950).

22 January

Lucky key: *D minor*
Enlightened religion: *Presbyterianism*
Favourite food: *cheese*

This will be the day in 2179 when Hikaru Walter Sulu, a character in *Star Trek*, will be born. He will find that he shares a birthday with Francis Bacon (1561), Lord Byron (1788) and Bill Bixby (1934), who played the pre-transformation Incredible Hulk.

Two famous women died on this day: Queen Victoria (1901) and Judy Garland (1969).

It's a good day for boxing: George Foreman beat Joe Frazier for the world heavyweight title in 1973, and in 1988 Mike Tyson knocked out Larry Holmes. More significantly, however, it was the day in 1859 when Brahms' First Piano Concerto (in D minor) had its first performance, in Hanover; in 1939 when the uranium atom was first split; in 1964 when the world's largest cheese was made in Wisconsin, weighing in at 15,723 kilograms (34,663 lb); and in 1882 when the Fifth Street Presbyterian Church of Troy, New York, became the first church in America to be lit by electric lighting.

23 January

Favourite food: *veal pie*
Beware of: *earthquakes*
Lucky royal gender: *female*

This was the birthday of the actors Humphrey Bogart (1899) and Randolph Scott (1903), and of the director Sergei Eisenstein (1898). As for painters, 23 January saw the birth of Édouard Manet (1832), but the deaths of Gustave Doré (1883), Edvard Munch (1944) and Salvador Dali (1989). On the whole, this makes the day worse for painting than for poetry, of which the only recorded loss was the death of Francisco Maldonado da Silva Solis, the Peruvian poet who was burnt at the stake on this date in 1639.

It is also the birthday of Charlotte Grand Duchess of Luxembourg (1896) and of Princess Caroline of Monaco (1957).

The worst earthquake in history happened on 23 January 1556, killing an estimated 830,000 people in Shensi province in China.

Quote of the day; 'My country! Oh, my country' or possibly 'I think I could eat one of Bellamy's veal pies' both of which have been cited as the last words of William Pitt the Younger in 1806.

24 January

Lucky profession: *king*
Unlucky orifice: *mouth*
Bad day for: *the Inuit*

Coincidence of the day: on 24 January 1918, the US television evangelist Oral Roberts was born, and 24 January 1989 saw the first reported case of AIDS transmitted by heterosexual oral sex.

This was the birthday of King Frederick II (the Great) of Prussia in 1712, and of King Gustav III of Sweden in 1746, while in 1236 Henry III of England married Eleanor of Provence.

In 1899 on this day, the rubber heel was patented by Humphrey O'Sullivan. In 1935, canned beer was first sold by the Krueger Brewing Co. in Richmond, Virginia. And in 1922 Eskimo Pie was patented by Christian K. Nelson of Iowa, who was not an Inuit.

Three film stars share this birthday: Sharon Tate (born 1943, murdered by Charles Manson), John Belushi (born 1949), and Nastassja Kinski (born 1960).

Other notable deaths on this date: Caligula (AD 41), Elsa the lioness (1961) and Winston Churchill (1965).

25 January

Burns Night

....

Lucky food: *haggis*
Lucky profession: *female priest*
Good day for: *the sun to shine*

Mendelssohn's 'Wedding March' was first performed on this day in 1858, at the marriage of Victoria, the Princess Royal (daughter of Queen Victoria), to Crown Prince Frederick of Prussia. It was an odd date to choose for a royal wedding, being also the day in 1533 when Henry VIII married Anne Boleyn, which did not turn out well at all.

Since 1886, this has been the date of the Saint Paul Carnival in Saint Paul, Minnesota. According to tradition, 'If the sun should shine on this day, a good year will follow.'

Notable births: Robert Burns (1759); Lord Lonsdale (Henry Cecil Lowther, 1857), who gave boxing its rules and Lonsdale belts.

Notable deaths: Al Capone (1947), Ava Gardner (1990).

Notable event: in 1944, Florence Tim-Oi Lee of Macao became the first Anglican female priest—a decision forced on the Church by the shortage of eligible men towards the end of the war.

---

26 January

Feast day of St Paula, patron saint of widows

....

Good day for: *dentistry*
Bad day for: *drugs and alcohol*
Unhappy day for: *eagles*

St Paula (347–404) was a Roman who married a senator called Toxotius, whose death left her a rich widow with five children at the age of about 33. She gave most of her money to charity and left her daughter St Eustochium, a dedicated virgin, in debt.

This is Australia Day and also Republic Day in India. The Australians celebrate the arrival in 1788 of Captain Arthur Phillips with a fleet of ships containing the first consignment of 736 convicts for the penal colony at Sydney Bay. India celebrates the day in 1950 when it became a democratic republic within the Commonwealth.

On this day in 1784, Benjamin Franklin expressed unhappiness over the choice of the eagle as America's symbol, while in 1875 George Green of Kalamazoo, Michigan, patented the battery-powered dentist's drill.

Other notable events: in 1838 Tennessee became the first state to ban alcohol; in 1956 the UK banned the import and export of heroin.

27 January

Good day for: *inventions*
Bad day for: *Germany*
Momentous day for: *music*

This was the date of birth, in 1859, of Kaiser Wilhelm II. On the Kaiser's 42nd birthday in 1901, his cousin King Edward VII made him a field marshal in the British army. His 63rd birthday coincided with the first congress of Adolf Hitler's Nazi Party in Munich.

More usefully for mankind, this was the day in 1880 when Thomas Edison patented the electric incandescent lamp, and the day in 1926 when John Logie Baird gave the first public demonstration of television.

Operatically, the date marks the birth of Wolfgang Amadeus Mozart in 1756 and the death of Giuseppe Verdi in 1901. The Broadway composer Jerome Kern also got in on the act by being born on this day in 1885. 27 January also marks the death of a man with a musical middle name: Sir Thomas Octave Sopwith, British aircraft designer renowned for his First World War biplane the Sopwith Camel.

One more birth: Lewis Carroll in 1832.

28 January

Favourite fruit: *banana*
Lucky number: *26*
Unlucky number: *2,443*

In 1447 on this day King Henry VII was born, exactly 100 years before King Henry VIII died. It is a worse day for emperors, however, having seen the deaths of Charlemagne in 814 and of the Holy Roman Emperor William of Holland in 1256.

This was the day in 1807 when Pall Mall in London became the first street in the world to be lit by gas lamps; in 1896 Walter Arnold of Kent was the first person to be fined for speeding (he was doing 8 mph in a 2 mph area); in 1935, Iceland became the first country to legalise abortion on sociomedical grounds; in 1946, the first bananas arrived in Britain since the war; in 1962, Johanne Relleke of Rhodesia was stung 2,443 times by bees and survived; and in 1984 in Las Vegas, Glynn Wolfe set a new record for non-bigamous marriages by marrying for the 26th time.

Missed opportunity of the day: in 1613 Galileo saw the undiscovered planet Neptune, but didn't realise what it was.

29 January

Auspicious profession: *petrol pump attendant*
Confusing day for: *eunuchs*
Favourite dessert: *cherry-flavoured ice-cream*

This was the day in 1886 when Karl Benz patented the first petrol-driven car. It was the birthday, in 1860, of Anton Chekhov, author of *The Cherry Orchard*, and the date in 1924 when Carl Taylor of Cleveland patented the ice-cream cone rolling machine.

On 29 January 1920 Walt Disney began his first job, earning $40 a week as an artist with the KC Slide Co. He celebrated the 39th anniversary of this occasion by releasing his full-length animated film of *Sleeping Beauty* on the same date in 1959.

Other notable birthdays include Germaine Greer, author of *The Female Eunuch*, in 1939, and Lawrence Hargrave, inventor of the box kite, in 1850.

In 1964 on this date, the Beatles recorded 'Komm, Gib Mir Deine Hand' and 'Sie Liebt Dich' ('I Wanna Hold Your Hand' and 'She Loves You') in German. In 1985, however, Oxford University dons voted against giving an honorary degree to Margaret Thatcher.

30 January

Bad day for: *heads of state*
Good day for: *scandal*
Successful activity: *assassination*

In 1649, Charles I was beheaded, for which the executioner was paid £30. In 1948, Mahatma Gandhi was assassinated. The Swedish prime minister Olof Palme, who was also to suffer assassination, was born on this day in 1927. And this was the date in 1965 of the state funeral of Winston Churchill.

Another head of state for whom this was a bad day was President von Hindenburg of Germany, who appointed Adolf Hitler chancellor in 1933. Six years later, to the day, Hitler called for the extermination of Jews.

It was the birthday in 1915 of John Profumo, the British war minister who was forced to resign after a scandal involving his dealings with a prostitute. He might never have been led astray had contraceptive pills not gone on sale in Britain on 30 January 1961.

Useful inventions on this date: bell chimes (1487), the pneumatic hammer (1894).

31 January

Lucky ailment: *venereal disease*
Lucky animal: *Arabian oryx*
Favourite food: *burger*

This was the birthday in 1797 of Franz Schubert, whose B minor symphony is known as the 'Unfinished' because that's what it is. He is believed to have died of syphilis at the age of 31, which was unfortunate bearing in mind that the first VD clinic had opened at the London Lock Hospital on 31 January 1747.

The most notable death on this day was that of Guy Fawkes, who was hanged, drawn and quartered in 1606.

In 1905, A. G. MacDonald became the first person to drive a car at more than 100 mph, yet we had to wait until the same day in 1983 for Britain to make seat-belts compulsory in front seats. It is a generally good day for the McDonald clan, with the first McDonald's in Russia (and the largest in the world) opening on this date in 1990.

Other notable events: in 1957, Liz Taylor's second divorce (from Michael Wilding) took place; in 1980, ten Arabian oryx were released into the wild in Oman—previously the animal had been extinct outside zoos.

---

1 February

Air Force Day in Nicaragua

Good day for: *going to the lavatory*
Not quite such a good day for: *pythons*
Lucky creature: *the ant*

Terry Jones (of *Monty Python*) was born on this day in 1943, but the same day in 1989 saw the death of Omiuri, a 16ft python believed by the Luo tribesmen of Kenya to have magical powers. Mary Shelley, creator of Frankenstein, died on this day in 1851, so the Kenyan snake is not the only monster associated with the date.

Ants can look back on the date with pleasure, having just squeezed into the first volume of the full *Oxford English Dictionary*, 'A–Ant', which was published on this day in 1884.

This is a good day for men, being the date in 1852 when the first men's public lavatory opened in London; and it's a good day for women, since 1 February 1973 was when it was voted that women brokers should be allowed on the floor of the London Stock Exchange.

Other notable birthdays: Clark Gable (1901), Sir Stanley Matthews (1915), Boris Yeltsin (1931).

2 February

Groundhog Day

This is a good day for getting up early and going to Punxsatawney, Philadelphia, to watch a groundhog named Punxsatawney Phil being lured out of its burrow. Legend has it that if it sees its shadow, it will scurry back into hibernation and winter will last another six weeks. If there is no shadow, then spring is just around the corner.

Other things that have happened on 2 February include:

1802: the first leopard is exhibited in the United States.
1880: the first frozen meat arrives in Great Britain from Sydney.
1935: for the first time a lie-detector is used as evidence in court.
1955: the first presidential news conference is shown on American TV.
1986: for the first time women are allowed to vote in Liechtenstein.
1977: for the first time residents of Rio de Janeiro have the opportunity to sell live cockroaches for $25 per 100 grams—the price offered by a medical laboratory researching new vaccines.

It was also the date in 1709 when Alexander Selkirk, on whom Robinson Crusoe was based, was rescued after four years and four months on Más a Tierra Island, where he had been shipwrecked.

3 February

Feast day of St Margaret, patron saint of pregnant women

Good day for: *manoeuvring*
Bad day for: *conducting*

According to legend, St Margaret burst out of the stomach of a dragon—a fine qualification for becoming patron saint of pregnancy.

Other women to celebrate include Elizabeth Blackwell (born on this day in 1821), Britain's first female physician, and Euphemia Alten, the 16-year-old composer of 'The Celebrated Chop Waltz' (commonly known as 'Chopsticks') which, under the pseudonym of Arthur de Lull, she registered at the British Museum on 3 February 1877.

Other notable anniversaries on this day include the first paper money in America, issued by the colony of Massachusetts in 1690; and the first soft landing (unmanned) on the moon, in 1966.

It was also the date of birth, in 1920, of Dr Henry Heimlich, inventor of the 'Heimlich manoeuvre' which was designed to prevent choking; and the day in 1958 when the Finnish composer Paavo Berglund broke his neck through over-vigorous head-shaking while conducting Usko Merilainen's piano concerto.

4 February

Favourite confectionery: *chewing-gum*
Unlucky garment: *underpants*
Beware of: *earthquakes*

This is an extraordinarily bad day for earthquakes. In Calabria, Italy, in 1783, some 50,000 people were killed in a quake; another one hit Quito, Ecuador, in 1797, killing an estimated 40,000; and in 1976 the death toll from an earthquake in Guatemala and Honduras was 22,778.

It is a good day for flying, being the date of birth in 1841 of Clément Ader, the Frenchman who was the first to fly a craft heavier than air, and also the birthday in 1902 of Charles Lindbergh, the first to fly solo across the Atlantic. In 1982, this same day saw a new world distance record of 47 metres for flying a paper aeroplane indoors.

Two notable events happened on this day in 1997 (which was, incidentally, the 50th birthday of former US vice-president Dan Quayle): archaeologists discovered that chewing-gum dates back to the Stone Age, and C&A withdrew 6,000 pairs of men's underpants from 120 stores because the hole was in the wrong place.

5 February

Japanese Martyrs' Day

Propitious profession: *actress*
Lucky item of clothing: *collar studs*
Favourite meal: *lunch*

In 1948 on this date Hezekiah Johnson, a road-sweeper in the English seaside town of Scarborough, fooled townsfolk into believing they had heard the first cuckoo of spring. Mr Johnson told his local paper: 'I wait until a crowd gathers at the bus-stop and then go into the park and do the cuckoo. I used to do the nightingale when I had my teeth in.'

This is the birthday of three noted actresses, Zsa Zsa Gabor (1917), Melina Mercouri (1923) and Charlotte Rampling (1946). It is also the birthday of William Burroughs, author of the novel *The Naked Lunch*.

The 12-year-old Charles Dickens started work in his first job on this day in 1824. He was paid six shillings a week for labelling bottles. Exactly one year later, Hannah Lord Montague of New York invented the first detachable collar.

6 February

Waitangi Day in New Zealand

....

Lucky game: *'Monopoly'*
Lucky sport: *golf*
Lucky vocation: *US president*

This is the birthday of a number of famous actors including Sir Henry Irving (1838) and Patrick Macnee (1922), John Steed in the television series *The Avengers*. But they are overshadowed by that even more famous actor Ronald Reagan (born in 1911), star of *Bedtime for Bonzo* and the White House.

Another president to have been lucky was Dwight Eisenhower, who hit a hole-in-one at golf on this day in 1968. And another golfer to have made his mark was Alan Shepard, who became the first person to hit a golf-ball on the moon on this date in 1971.

This was the day in 1665 that Queen Anne was born, and the day in 1952 that King George VI died. Most significant of all, however, it was the day in 1997 when it was reported that St Petersburg had opened Russia's first kick-boxing school for nannies, to counter the growing problem of child-kidnapping.

---

7 February

Independence Day in Grenada

....

Lucky complex: *inferiority*
Unlucky fish: *sardine*
Eventful day for: *Walt Disney*

In 1639 on this day, the Académie Française began compiling its first dictionary of the French language. In addition, one of the greatest writers in the English language, Charles Dickens, was born on this date in 1812, which was also the day that Lord Byron made his maiden speech in the House of Lords. Another notable birthday today was that of Alfred Adler, the psychiatrist who introduced the concept of the inferiority complex.

Walt Disney's full-length cartoon feature *Snow White and the Seven Dwarfs* was given an 'A' certificate (children admitted only if accompanied by adults) by the British film censors on this day in 1938, because the wicked witch was considered too frightening. Unperturbed, Disney released *Pinocchio* on this day in 1940.

In 1989, it rained sardines over Ipswich, Australia—the fish had probably been lifted from the sea by an updraught.

---

8 February

Narvik Sun Pageant Day in Norway

Good day for: *executions*
Bad day for: *adultery*
Luck profession: *actress*

Mary, Queen of Scots, was beheaded on this day in 1587, and in 1924, at Nevada State Prison, Gee Jon became the first person to be put to death in a gas chamber in the USA.

In 1939 on this day, the House of Lords passed the Bastardy Bill, making blood-tests compulsory in paternity suits.

If this is your birthday, you should consider becoming an actress: Dame Edith Evans (1885), Lana Turner (1920) and Brooke Adams (1949) were all born on this day. So was Jules Verne (1828).

The earth moved for Londoners on this day in 1750, when a slight earthquake was recorded, and in 1977 a tremor registering 5.0 on the Richter scale was felt in San Francisco. The biggest earth movement, however, appeared to have happened on 8 February 1996 when scientists monitoring the satellite-based Global Positioning System discovered that the South Pole was 18 inches away from where they thought it was.

9 February

Feast day of St Apollonia, patron saint of toothache-sufferers

Momentous day for: *horse-racing*
Lucky part of the body: *fallopian tube*
Favourite vegetable *asparagus*

This is a very good day for hitting a ball over a net. On 9 February 1895, the game of volleyball was invented by W. G. Morgan of Massachusetts, and on the same day in 1900 Dwight F. Davis inaugurated the Davis Cup for tennis.

This is a day for both rejoicing and dismay among race-goers: it was the date in 1540 of the first recorded horse-race meeting in the UK, which took place in Chester, and the day in 1983 of the kidnapping of the Grand National winner Shergar.

Other important events include the arrival in San Francisco of the first shipment of asparagus from Sacramento (1891); the first (amateur) striptease, performed by Mona, an artist's model, at the Four Arts Ball at the Moulin Rouge (1893); Greta Garbo becoming a US citizen (1951); and the first successful transplant of a fallopian tube in the UK (1979).

10 February

Feast day of St Scholastica, virgin and patron saint of convulsive children

Favourite metal: *gold*
Good day for: *marriage*
Bad day for: *a sea voyage*

This is said to have been the day in AD 60 when St Paul was shipwrecked off Malta. As hazards go, it bodes ill for fire, since 10 February 1863 was when the first patent for a fire-extinguisher was granted to Alanson Crane of Virginia.

Two notable marriages occurred on this date: in 1840 Queen Victoria married Prince Albert, and in 1863 Tom Thumb married Mercy Lavinia Warren in a special ceremony organised at P. T. Barnum's Circus. Neither of the gentlemen involved would therefore have been subject to the tax on bachelors which Wisconsin passed on this date in 1905.

On 10 February 1942 the first gold disc was awarded to Glenn Miller for his recording of 'Chattanooga Choo Choo'. Another golden connection is provided by Mark Spitz, winner of nine Olympic swimming gold medals, born on this date in 1950.

11 February

National Inventors' Day in the USA

Lucky profession: *weather forecaster*
Unlucky profession: *wig-maker*

This was the birthday in 1847 of Thomas Alva Edison, whose 1,093 patents include the electric light-bulb and the phonograph. The photography pioneer William Fox Talbot, however, may claim to have got there before him, having been born on the same day in 1800.

It is a good day for sex, being the date of birth in 1925 of Virginia Johnson who, as half of Masters and Johnson, has devoted most of her life to researching this important topic. It was also, in 1936, the birthday of Burt Reynolds, who became the first male centrefold in *Playgirl* magazine. More finally, it was the day in 1650 when René ('I think therefore I am') Descartes stopped thinking and wasn't any more.

In 1765 on this day, wig-makers begged George III for financial compensation because wigs had gone out of fashion; and in 1878, the British meteorological office started giving weekly weather forecasts. In 1997 a court in Papua New Guinea ruled against the practice of using young women as payment in compensation cases.

12 February

Bad day for: *a snowball fight*
Confusing day for: *tortoises*
Lucky number: *200358*

Both Abraham Lincoln and Charles Darwin were born on this day in 1809. On their 22nd birthday, in 1831, J. W. Goodrich first marketed rubber galoshes. Baseball-players could therefore have played for 47 years in galoshes before the first catcher's mask was patented by Frederick Thayer (pat. no. 200358) on this day in 1878.

This was the day in 1879 when North America gained its first artificial ice-rink, and the day in 1984 when at the Winter Olympics Torvill and Dean received a full set of perfect scores for ice-dancing to Ravel's *Bolero*. It was also the day in 1996 when children in Skokie, Illinois, had a marshmallow fight with 230,000 marshmallows. They had hoped to break the record for the world's largest snowball fight, but it didn't snow, so they used marshmallows instead.

Finally, this was the day in 1997 when Australian scientists first announced their discovery that the Fitzroy River tortoise, *Rheodytes leukops*, breathes through its mouth on land and through its bottom under water.

13 February

Your lucky number: *1,286*
Your favourite pastime: *making love*
Your unlucky disease: *cholera*

This is a day of ill omen: in 1542 Catherine Howard, fifth wife of Henry VIII, was beheaded; in 1832, the first outbreak of cholera in London was recorded; in 1883, Richard Wagner died; in 1971, the US vice-president Spiro Agnew hit three spectators with his first two tee-shots when playing in the Bob Hope Desert Golf Classic; and in 1974, Alexander Solzhenitsyn was expelled from the USSR.

On a more positive note, it was also the birthday, in 1903, of the crime novelist and creator of Maigret, George Simenon, who claimed to have made love to more than 10,000 women. On a similar theme, it was also the day in 1998 when Greek archaeologists unearthed a 2,000-year-old phallus on the site of what was believed to have been the world's oldest brothel in Salonika.

In 1959 on this day the Barbie Doll first went on sale, and in 1981 the New York *Times* published a 1,286-word sentence, its longest ever.

14 February

Day of National Mourning in Mexico

Lucky country: *United States*
Favourite kitchen utensil: *apple-parer*
Worst holiday venue: *Hawaii*

On this day in 1477, Margery Brews sent a card to John Paston in Norfolk addressed 'to my right welbelovyd voluntyne'—the earliest-known Valentine's Day greeting. In a more modern spirit of romance, it was the day in 1989 when Mike Tyson and Robin Givens divorced.

This is an important day in the history of America: in 1803, Moses Coats of Pennsylvania patented the apple-parer; in 1848, James K. Polk became the first president photographed in office; in 1859 George Washington Gale Ferris, inventor of the ferris wheel, was born; in 1889, the first trainload of oranges left Los Angeles for the east of the country; and in 1929 seven members of Bugs Moran's gang were killed in the St Valentine's Day massacre. Two states joined the union on this day: Oregon in 1859 and Arizona in 1912.

In 1779, this was the day when natives of Hawaii killed Captain James Cook.

15 February

Good day for: *music*
Bad day for: *Britain*
Mixed day for: *physics*

In 1564 on this day one of the greatest physicist/astronomers of the sixteenth century, Galileo Galilei, was born, and in 1988 Richard Feynman, one of the greatest twentieth-century physicists, died.

A notable birthday in the history of the pianoforte was that of Henry Engelhard Steinway in 1797, while on exactly the same date in 1965 John Lennon passed his driving test.

Britain chose this date in 1971 to change to decimal currency after 1,200 years of pounds, shillings and pence. Seven years later, on 15 February 1978, England lost to New Zealand for the first time at cricket—an appropriate result, perhaps, for it was on this day in 1882 that the first frozen meat shipment left New Zealand for England.

Other notable events on this day: in 1903 the first teddy-bear went on sale in the United States; in 1925 Regent's Park Zoo in London announced that lights would be installed to cheer up the animals on foggy days.

16 February

Independence Day in Lithuania

Good day to: *make a journey*
Wearing: *nylon stockings*
Paying: *by cheque*

In 1914 the first ever flight from San Francisco to Los Angeles was made on this date. Only 46 years later, in 1960, the nuclear submarine US *Triton* began the first ever journey around the world under water. Between these two events, on the same day in 1924 Howard Carter raised the lid of Tutankhamun's sarcophagus; James Markham received the first patent for a tree, for his breeding of a peach tree in 1932; nylon was patented in the USA by a team led by Dr Wallace Hume Carothers in 1937; in 1956 Britain abolished the death penalty; and in 1997 scientists at the University of Connecticut discovered that disliking broccoli is a genetically inherited trait.

Further back in time, this was the day in 1568 when the Spanish Inquisition sentenced the whole of the Netherlands to death, and the day in 1659 when the first British cheque, for £400, was drawn by Nicholas Vanacker.

---

17 February

Good day to: *eat chocolate-covered sardines by gaslight behind the locked door of a lavatory cubicle*

In 1673 on this day the great French playwright Molière died, and in 1856 the German poet Heinrich Heine. To compensate a little, it was the birthday in 1781 of René Laënnec, inventor of the stethoscope, in 1867 of the great chocolate-maker William Cadbury, in 1908 of the Apache chief Geronimo, in 1929 of the Palestinian leader Yasser Arafat, and in 1934 of Barry Humphries, creator of Dame Edna Everidge.

In 1972 the Volkswagen Beetle overtook the Model T Ford as the most prolific car of all time as its 15,007,034th model rolled off the production line. On the same day, significantly enough, the British parliament voted to join the Common Market.

In 1817 on this date, Baltimore became the first US city to be lit by gas; in 1876 the first tin of sardines was produced in Eastport, Maine; and in 1883 Mr A. Ashwell of Herne Hill in south London patented the Vacant/Engaged sign for lavatory doors.

18 February

National Bun Day in Iceland

Bad habit: *snoring*
Unlucky wine: *malmsey*
Good day to: *publish a book*

If you were born on this day, your chances of having a scientific unit named after you are better than average. Count Alessandro Volta (born today in 1745), who invented the battery, gave his name to the volt, and the Austrian physicist Ernst Mach (born 1838) became a unit of air speed: Mach 1 is the speed of sound.

In 1678, John Bunyan's *Pilgrim's Progress* was published, and Mark Twain chose the same day in 1884 to publish *Huckleberry Finn*.

It was a good day for music in 1894 when the guitarist Andrés Segovia was born, but a bad day for art in 1564 when Michelangelo died.

In 1478 on this day, George, Duke of Clarence, was murdered in the Tower of London by being drowned in a butt of malmsey, and on 18 February 1997 an Iranian was reported to have filed for divorce on the grounds of his wife's snoring. In the 40 days of their marriage, she had given him sleeping pills with dinner to prevent him discovering her bad habit.

19 February

Lucky profession: *wig-maker*
Lucky number: *200521*
Lucky waterway: *creek*

In 1897 on this day, two remarkable things happened: Charles Blondin, the French tight-rope walker, was born, and Mrs Hoodless founded the Women's Institute at Stoney Creek, Ontario. This is not the only creek with reason to remember the day, for in 1906 William K. Kellogg founded the Battle Creek Toasted Corn Flake Company to market the breakfast food invented by his brother, John Harvey Kellogg. Cornflakes had originally been devised as therapy for mental patients and as a way of curbing sex drive.

In 1878, patent number 200521 was assigned to Thomas Edison's phonograph and exactly three years later Kansas became the first state to prohibit the sale of alcohol. In 1964, the Beatle look became so popular in the United States that half a ton of Beatle wigs were flown from the UK to the USA on this day.

Notable births include Philip V of Spain (1683), William III of the Netherlands (1817) and Prince Andrew of Great Britain (1960).

20 February

John Glenn Day in the USA

....

Good day for: *Batman and Robin*
Bad day for: *Donald Duck*
Lucky implement: *toothpick*

In 1962 on this day, John Glenn became the first American to orbit the earth. More significantly for most people, it was the day in 1939 when nylon stockings first went on sale in New York and the day in 1985 when the sale of contraceptives became legal in the Irish Republic.

On 20 February 1944 a *Batman and Robin* comic strip first appeared in newspapers; and in 1985 Clarence Nash, who had provided the voice for Donald Duck, died at the age of 80.

In 1811 on this day, Austria announced that the country was bankrupt, and in 1839 the US Congress banned duelling in the District of Columbia. Other notable events include the first wine auction in London (1673) and the first toothpick-manufacturing machine patented in the USA (1872).

Famous births: Alexei Kosygin (1904), Cindy Crawford (1966).

21 February

....

Auspicious hobby: *photography*
Lucky country: *Liechtenstein*
Unlucky profession: *burglar*

This day has seen a wide variety of firsts: in 1842, John Greenough was granted the first American patent for a sewing-machine; in 1858 Edwin Holmes of Boston, Massachusetts, was the first person to install an electric burglar alarm. This same day in 1925 saw the first issue of the *New Yorker* magazine.

Photography can claim two important firsts for this day, with the camera exposure meter patented in 1932 and the first instant camera (later known as the Polaroid) demonstrated by its inventor E. H. Land in 1947. Exactly five years later, on 21 February 1952, Dick Button became the first figure-skater to execute a triple jump in competition.

Most important of all, this was the day in 1980 when Hanni Weizel won the giant slalom to give Liechtenstein its first ever Olympic gold medal.

Significant death: ballerina Margot Fonteyn in 1991.

22 February

Donkey Races Day in the Virgin Islands

Significant country: *United States*
Bad day for: *invading England*
Lucky religion: *Jewish*

In 1512 on this day, the Italian navigator Amerigo Vespucci, after whom America was named, died; and in 1732 George Washington was born. This was also the date of the first organised baseball match in the USA in 1860, and the date in 1935 on which aeroplanes were banned from flying over the White House.

It is also a highly significant day for Britain, marking the last time the British mainland was invaded by foreign troops. It happened in 1797 when 1,400 French soldiers described as 'the scum of every gaol in France' landed at Fishguard in Wales from a fleet of convict ships. They surrendered two days later when they mistook Welsh women in national dress for British troops.

Quote of the day: 'Because I love all this Jewish stuff' —Harvey Penson on 22 February 1998, when asked why he was celebrating his bar mitzvah on the eve of his 93rd birthday.

23 February

Recommended vocation: *US president*
Good day for: *not being hanged*
Bad day for: *polygamy*

This was the birthday of two US presidents, John Quincy Adams (1767) and Woodrow Wilson (1856). If you are not American and are therefore ineligible for the presidency, an alternative career to consider might be that of opera composer, for it was also the date of birth of John Blow (1649), whose *Venus and Adonis* was the first opera in English, and of George Frideric Handel (1685).

Painting and poetry have fared less well today, with the deaths of Sir Joshua Reynolds in 1792 and John Keats in 1821. Another to die on this day was the Frenchman Henri Landau, executed for having eleven wives. He was less lucky than John Lee who, on this day in 1885, survived three attempts to hang him at Exeter Prison when the trap-door failed to open. Lee was released in 1917 and died in 1933.

In 1919 on this day Mussolini founded the Fascist Party of Italy, and in 1956 the West German army banned the goose-step.

24 February

Good day for: *starting a war*
Expensive day for: *buying a pig*
Inauspicious day for: *getting engaged*

This was the day in 1582 when the world began to get the date right: Pope Gregory XIII announced the change from the Julian to the Gregorian calendar.

In 1836 on this date, the Mexican army began its siege of the Alamo. This appears to have started a trend, because on the same day in 1895 the Cuban War of Independence began, in 1917 the Russian Revolution broke out, in 1948 there was a Communist coup in Czechoslovakia, and in 1991 the coalition forces began their ground war to drive Iraq out of Kuwait.

In 1839 William Otis of Philadelphia patented the steam shovel.

In 1979 a pig was sold in Stamford, Texas, for $42,500—a new world record price.

In 1981 Prince Charles and Lady Diana Spencer announced their engagement and 13 years later, on 24 February 1994, British Coal announced the retirement of its last four working pit-ponies.

25 February

Lucky vegetable: *potato*
Lucky fruit: *orange*
Beware of: *bananas*

In 1922 on this day, Donald McLean was born. He was to become Scotland's greatest potato expert with the world's largest private collection numbering 367 varieties. It was also the birthday, in 1917, of Anthony Burgess, author of *A Clockwork Orange*.

The same day in 1946 saw the first post-war sale of bananas to the British public. A girl in Bridlington ate four of them and died.

On 25 February 1998, Switzerland's first legal brothel opened in Zurich.

Quote of the day:

> Here we are sitting together in the nude.
> Some folks in society would exclaim to us how rude!
> But we know we're all good people, we came to praise the Lord,
> So let's all shout to Jesus and clap our hands of one accord.

—Carol Love at the opening of the First Nudist Conference at Whispering Pines Resort, California, 25 February 1997.

26 February

Good day for: *looking out*
Terrible day for: *buffalo*
Lucky operation: *kidney transplant*

This was the birthday in 1846 of William 'Buffalo Bill' Cody, who earned his nickname by killing 4,280 buffalo. To add indignity to slaughter, this was also the day in 1891 when the first buffalo was purchased for the Golden Gate Park in San Francisco.

It was also the birthday, in 1361, of King Wenceslas of Bohemia, famed for looking out on the feast of Stephen. Looking out, however, would not have helped the 20,000 inhabitants of Lisbon who were killed on this day in 1531 by a severe earthquake.

Notable events of the day include the first issue of a pound note by the Bank of England (1797), the first televised kidney transplant (1975), and the rejection by the Peruvian Congress of a bill to ban miniskirts in the workplace (1998). It was also the day in 1997 when Larry Blanchfield, 31, a prisoner at Delaware Correctional Centre, was crushed to death when he tried to escape in a garbage truck.

27 February

Recommended profession: *writer*
Good day for: *a wedding*
Bad day for: *rolling your own cigar*

This is an interesting day for music, marking the death in 1887 of the great Russian composer Alexander Borodin; the first performance, in 1800, of Beethoven's First Symphony; and the day in 1883 when that great writer of musicals, Oscar Hammerstein, received a patent for his invention of the cigar-rolling machine.

Generally writers and poets have fared even better than musicians on this day, since it saw the births of Henry Wadsworth Longfellow in 1807, John Steinbeck in 1902 and Lawrence Durrell in 1912.

In 1557 on this day the first Russian embassy opened in London, and in 1897 a wedding in Paris saw the couple leave in the world's first decorated wedding car. One hundred years later, on 27 February 1997, Singapore extended its ban on nudity in public to private places in public view.

Elizabeth Taylor was born today, in 1932.

28 February

Kalevala Day in Finland

Favoured means of transport: *bicycle*
Favourite composer: *Schubert*
Unlucky drink: *Coca-Cola*

Besides being the day in 1819 when a Schubert song was first performed in public (nine years before his death), the day in 1970 when cycling was first permitted across the Golden Gate Bridge in San Francisco, and the day in 1950 when Paris passed a bill curbing the sale of Coca-Cola, this was also the date in 1912 when the House of Lords passed a bill saying that husbands may no longer be deemed to have coerced wives who commit offences in their presence.

It was also the birthday in 1903 of Vincente Minnelli, famous film-director father of a still more famous daughter, Liza; and it was the birthday in 1926 of Svetlana Alliluyeva, famous daughter of an even more famous father, Joseph Stalin.

Two Nobel Prize winners share this birthday: Linus Pauling (born 1901), winner for Chemistry in 1954 and for Peace in 1962, and Peter Medawar (born 1915), winner for Physiology or Medicine in 1960.

29 February

Commemoration of St Hilarius, calendar reformer

Lucky sport: *rowing*
Lucky profession *Pope*
Lucky animal: *bunny*

For a day that only comes along 97 times every 400 years, 29 February has many religious connotations. It marked the death of Pope Hilarius in 468, and the birth of Pope Paul III exactly 1,000 years later. It was also the date of the deaths of St Oswald, Bishop of York, in 992, and John Whitgift, Archbishop of Canterbury, in 1604.

Less religiously, it was the date in 1960 when Hugh Hefner opened his first Playboy Club in Chicago, scantily clad bunnies and all. In 1504 on this day, Christopher Columbus used his knowledge of an impending lunar eclipse to frighten the native Jamaicans.

Others who had birthdays only once in four years include Gioacchino Rossini (whose misfortune in being born on 29 February 1792 meant that his second true birthday did not occur until he was 12, since 1800 was not a leap year) and Nikolai and Yuri Pimenov (born 1948), silver-medallists in the Olympic coxless pairs in 1976.

1 March

New Year's Day in ancient Rome

Good day for: *celestial bodies*
Favourite garment: *shorts*
Unlucky drink: *rum*

On this day in 1966 the Soviet space probe Venus III landed on Venus, the first craft to land on another planet. It was an appropriate moment to choose, being the date of birth of Harry Belafonte (1927), who starred in the 1957 film *Island in the Sun*, and of David Niven (1910), who entitled the first volume of his autobiography *The Moon's a Balloon*.

This was the start of the first month of the Julian calendar in ancient Rome, which is why we call September, October, November and December after the Latin words for seven, eight, nine and ten.

In 1784 on this date E. Kidner opened Britain's first cookery school, and in 1990 the Royal New Zealand Navy became the world's last navy to scrap the daily rum ration.

Quote of the day: 'I can see no reason why women should not wear shorts' —the Prince of Wales, later Edward VIII, on 1 March 1934.

2 March

Peasants' Day in Burma

Recommended profession: *Pope*
Lucky number: *365*
Recommended journey: *round the world*

In 1949 on this day, the plane *Lucky Lady II* of the US Air Force completed the first non-stop round-the-world flight after several mid-air refuellings from tanker aircraft. On the same day Dame Naomi James was born, who was to become the first woman to sail round the world single-handed. An undeniably shorter but possibly less taxing journey would be a trip round Disney World, for it was on this day in 1976 that Disney World received its 50-millionth visitor.

This is also the birthday of two popes, Leo XIII (1810) and Pius XII (1876), and of one cardinal, Basil Hume (1923). If you were born on this day but do not want to become Pope, an alternative career as an American novelist beckons, for this was also the date of birth of Tom Wolfe (1931) and of John Irving (1942).

And it was the day in 1958 when Gary Sobers scored 365 not out against Pakistan at Kingston, Jamaica, a record that stood for over 35 years.

3 March

Japanese Girls' Day in Hawaii

Favoured form of transport: *train*
Testing form of transport: *bicycle*
Lucky art form: *music*

Beethoven's 'Moonlight Sonata' was first performed on this day in 1802; 73 years later, on 3 March 1875, Bizet's *Carmen* had its première at the Opéra Comique in Paris; and on the same date in 1931 'The Star-spangled Banner' became the US national anthem.

Great men who were born today include Alexander Graham Bell (1847), inventor of the telephone, and George Pullman (1831), inventor of the railway sleeping-car. This comfortable mode of transport must have come as good news to people in Munich, where 'driving tests' for cyclists were instituted on this day in 1895.

Heads of state have had varied fortunes on this date. In 1904, Kaiser Wilhelm of Germany became the first person to have a political speech recorded on an Edison cylinder, and in 1991 Queen Elizabeth II needed three stitches in a finger after she had tried to break up a fight between two of her corgi dogs.

4 March

Good day for: *having a birthday*
Bad day for: *whipping children*
Lucky fruit: *orange*

In 1809 on this day, James Madison became the first US president to wear clothes made in America at his inauguration. Ninety-nine years later, on 4 March 1908, the New York Board of Education banned the use of whips in schools. Still in America, this was the day in 1792 when oranges were introduced to Hawaii and the day in 1849 when Senator David Atchison became president for a day. James Polk's term had ended on a Sunday and Zachary Taylor (born in Orange county, Virginia) could not be sworn in until the following day.

Notable births include the composer Antonio Vivaldi (1678), the psychologist Hans Eysenck (1916) and the astronomer Patrick Moore (1923). The last of these may have arrived just in time to have 'Happy Birthday to You' sung to him on his first birthday, for that was the day the song was published by Clayton F. Summy.

Quote of the day: 'We're more popular than Jesus Christ right now' — John Lennon, 4 March 1966.

5 March

Favourite food: *noodles*
Good day for: *precision*
Lucky relative: *mother-in-law*

This was the date of birth of two of the most precise men born in the sixteenth century: Gerardus Mercator (1512), the leading geographer and map-maker of his time, and William Oughtred (1575), inventor of the slide rule.

It is a good day for mothers-in-law, being the day in 1934 that Mother-in-law's Day was first celebrated in Amarillo, Texas. On the other hand, it's a bad day for dogs, for in 1986 on this day villagers in Malacca, Malaysia, beat to death a dog that was believed to be one of a gang of thieves who transformed themselves into animals.

More positively, this was the day in 1997 of the creation of IRMA — the Instant Ramen Manufacturers' Association, for noodle-makers, at the World Ramen Summit in Tokyo.

Notable death: Joseph Stalin in 1953.

Quote of the day: 'An iron curtain has descended over Europe' — Winston Churchill, speaking in Fulton, Missouri, on 5 March 1946.

6 March

Stoneware Pottery Appreciation Day in the USA; Magellan Day in Guam

Good day for: *having a headache while listening to the wireless, wearing glasses and eating frozen squirrel pie*

In 1899 on this day, Felix Hoffman patented Aspirin. Three years later, on 6 March 1902, the British army permitted soldiers to wear spectacles off duty. In 1924 on this day, Pius XI became the first pope to have a wireless installed at the Vatican; in 1930 frozen foods, developed by Clarence Birdseye, first went on sale in Massachusetts; and in 1946 the British food ministry issued a recipe for squirrel pie.

In 1844 the Russian composer Nicholas Rimsky-Korsakov was born, followed, exactly a hundred years later, by the opera singer Dame Kiri te Kanawa. This was also the day in 1521 when Magellan discovered Guam and the day in 1964 when Cassius Clay changed his name to Muhammad Ali.

Other important births: Michelangelo (1475), Cyrano de Bergerac (1619) and the inventor of the flop, Dick Fosbury (1947).

7 March

....

Good day for: *women*
Bad day for: *women drivers*
Unlucky organ: *penis*

On this day in 1908 the mayor of Cincinnati said that women were not physically fit to drive cars; all the same, the Swiss gave women the right to vote and hold federal office on the same day in 1971.

Whether drivers or non-drivers, women probably had very little to do with the Ivory Coast mobs who, on this day in 1997, beat to death two alleged sorcerers whom they had accused of making men's penises shrink or disappear. In mitigation, those responsible could have pointed out that it was the 16th anniversary of the date in 1981 when the first homicide was recorded at Disneyland.

In 1911 on this day, Willis Farnsworth of California patented the coin-operated locker, and in 1933 Clarence Darrow modified the rules of a game called 'The Landlord's Game' to give us 'Monopoly'.

Notable deaths: Aristotle (322 BC), Thomas Aquinas (1274).

---

8 March

Feast day of St John of God, patron saint of booksellers

....

Lucky tree: *willow*
Inauspicious vocation: *US president*
Notable day for: *moles*

In 1702 on this day, William III died after being thrown from his horse when it stumbled on a molehill in the grounds of Hampton Court. And in 1859 Kenneth Grahame was born, author of *The Wind in the Willows*, in which Mole, friend of Mr Toad, was to play a similarly important role.

It is also a significant day in the history of the rivalry between the USA and the USSR. The Americans got off to a bad start with the deaths of two presidents on this day—Millard Fillmore in 1874 and William Taft in 1930—then in 1950, the USSR announced that it had its own atom bomb. The situation escalated on the same date in 1965 when the first American troops arrived in Vietnam, and in 1983, again on 8 March, President Reagan called the USSR an 'evil empire'.

This was a sad day in 1959, when the Marx Brothers, Groucho, Chico and Harpo, made their last television appearance together.

9 March

....

Bad day for: *kissing*
Good day for: *going into space*
Sad day for: *interior decoration*

The first man in space, Yuri Gagarin, was born on this day in 1934. To celebrate his 27th birthday in 1961, the USSR put the first dog into space. The most significant extraterrestrial achievement on this day, however, was the discovery of the first volcano in space on Io, a moon of Jupiter, in 1979.

Kissing was banned in Naples on penalty of death on this date in 1562, but that did not deter Napoleon from marrying Josephine on the same day in 1796. This was the birthday in 1454 of Amerigo Vespucci, who gave America its name, and in 1943 of Bobby Fischer, who brought America the world chess championship. In 1988, though, it was the day that Richard C. Adams, inventor of the paint-roller, died.

Two other notable inventions have a claim to this day: in 1876 Alexander Graham Bell patented the telephone, and in 1822 Charles Graham of New York patented false teeth.

10 March

....

Ideal profession: *Soviet Olympic gold-medallist*
Good day to: *make a phone call*
Excellent day for: *dogs*

In 1886 on this day, the first Cruft's Dog Show opened in London, and on the same day in 1975 dog spectacles were patented.

Three Russian Olympic gold-medallists were born on this day: Anatoly Roschlin (1932), who won the super-heavyweight wrestling in 1972, Tamara Press (1937), winner of the women's shotput in 1960 and 1964, and her sister Irina Press (1939), who won the 80-metre hurdles in 1960 and the pentathlon in 1964.

Equally competitively, this was the day in 1974 when the last Japanese soldier of the Second World War surrendered. He was found on Lubang Island in the Philippines, unaware that the war had ended.

Discovery of the day: in 1996 scientists in Chicago revealed that women who drink coffee are less likely to commit suicide than those who don't.

Quote of the day: 'Come here, Watson, I want you'—the first telephone call made on 10 March 1876 by Alexander Graham Bell.

11 March

Johnny Appleseed Day in the USA

Your lucky city: *Rome*
Your lucky composer: *Verdi*
Your favourite type of flour: *self-raising*

In William Shakespeare's *Romeo and Juliet*, this was the date in the year 1302 of the young lovers' wedding. In 1986, the same day marked the passage of a million days since the legendary founding of Rome in 753 BC.

This has been a good day for lovers of Verdi, marking the first performance of *Rigoletto* in 1851 and of *Don Carlos* in 1867. It was a significant day for newspapers, too, with the publication of England's first daily paper, the *Daily Courant*, in 1702, and the birth of Rupert Murdoch in 1931.

Other notable birthdays include Frederick IX of Denmark (1899), Harold Wilson (1916), and Douglas Adams (1952). This was also the day in 1985 when Mikhail Gorbachev became Soviet leader, the date in 1892 of the first public basketball game and the day in 1845 when Henry Jones invented self-raising flour.

12 March

A good day for: *chanting*
While wearing a: *tutu*
Miraculous vegetable: *aubergine*

This was the date in 604 of the death of Pope Gregory, the saint who gave his name to Gregorian chant.

It was the birthday, in 1832, of the Irish estate manager Charles Boycott, who gave his name to a policy of avoidance after he had refused to lower rents after crop failure and famine; leading politicians recommended that no one should communicate with him—a 'boycott Boycott' policy, one might say. The Russian ballet dancer Vaslav Nijinsky was also born today, in 1890 (and he had a great race-horse named after him). Another connection with ballet relates to 1832, when 12 March saw the first appearance on stage of a tutu.

On this day in 1913 Canberra became the capital of Australia, and exactly five years later Moscow became the capital of Russia. On 12 March 1996, a group of British Muslims in Bolton were reported to have proclaimed a miracle after finding the word 'Allah' spelt out in the seeds inside an aubergine.

13 March

Good day for: *discovering a planet*
Lucky element: *oxygen*
Beware of: *cold ears*

Sir William Herschel discovered Uranus on this day in 1781 and named it Georgius Sidus after King George III. In honour of Herschel, Clyde Tombaugh waited until the same date in 1930 to announce his own discovery of Pluto.

In 1770 on this day, Daniel Lambert was born in Leicester. He grew to weigh 335 kilos (739 lb), had a 260 cm (102 in) waist, and it took 20 men to lift him into his grave. By contrast, the same day in 1894 witnessed the first professional strip-tease, an act called 'Le Coucher d'Yvette' at the Divan Payonau in Paris.

Other anniversaries: in 1733 Joseph Priestley, the discovered of oxygen, was born; in 1887 Chester Greenwood of Maine patented ear-muffs; in 1894, J. L. Johnstone invented the horse-race starting-gate; and in 1996 Abelardo Cachique Rivera protested at being given a 12-year-sentence for drug dealing in Peru, saying: 'It's too low a sentence, given my status as a major drug trafficker.'

14 March

Good day to: *encourage the others*
Liberated day for: *lionesses*
Lucky fabric: *cotton*

This was the day in 1757 when Admiral John Byng was shot by firing squad for failing in his duty of relieving Minorca from attack by the French. It was Byng's execution that inspired Voltaire's memorable expression, 'pour encourager les autres'.

Others who did not carry out their duty on this day were the 1939 English cricket team, who abandoned play on the 12th day of their match against South Africa—the longest ever test match—in order not to miss their boat home.

In 1923, this was the day that President Harding became the first US president to file an income tax return; and in 1985 five lionesses at Singapore Zoo were put on the contraceptive pill because of a large rise in the lion population over the preceding years.

Notable births today include Albert Einstein (1879) and Michael Caine (1933). The most notable death was that of Karl Marx in 1883. The most useful invention was Eli Whitney's cotton gin in 1793.

15 March

Thanksgiving Day in Honduras

Good day for: *a blood transfusion*
Worrying day for: *matter*
Beware: *the Ides of March*

On this day in 44 BC Julius Caesar was assassinated by Brutus, Cassius and others in the Senate House in Rome. Perhaps thinking of Caesar's fate, Leon Trotsky chose this date in 1929 to announce that he was giving up politics, but it didn't save him from assassination.

More positively, this was the day in 1892 that Jesse Reno of Chicago patented the 'Reno inclined elevator', the first escalator. But more negatively, it was also the day in 1962 when five distinct groups of scientists announced the discovery of antimatter.

In 1937 on this day, America's first state contraceptive clinic opened in Raleigh, North Carolina, and the first US blood bank was set up at Cook County Hospital. Its founder, Bernard Faustus, was the man who coined the term 'blood bank'.

Achievement of the day: Charles Bannerman scored the first ever test century, for England against Australia at Melbourne in 1877.

16 March

Feast day of St Urho, patron saint of Finland, who never existed

Greatest asset: *longevity*
Innovative gender: *female*
Bad day for: *going outside*

This date has strong connections with centenarians, for it was the day of birth in 1849 of the Reverend James E. Smith, who went on to become a father at the age of 100 with a woman 64 years his junior. It was also the day in 1959 when John Sailling, the last surviving veteran of the American Civil War, died—at the age of 111.

Caroline Herschel, the first notable woman astronomer, was born on 16 March 1750; and on the same day in New York in 1876, Nelly Saunders and Rose Harland took part in the first official women's boxing match.

In 1888, this day saw the first recorded sale of a motor car (to Émile Roger of Paris); it was also the 52nd birthday of Andrew S. Hallidie, the inventor of the cable car.

Quote of the day: 'I am just going outside and may be some time'— Lawrence Oates, 16 March 1912.

17 March

Feast day of Gertrude of Nivelle, patron saint of the recently dead

....

Good day for: *staying out of the rain*
Bad day for: *woodpeckers*
Momentous day for: *anyone named Roosevelt*

According to the nineteenth-century theologian Gustav Seyffarth, this was the date in 3446 BC when Noah entered the Ark. Other notable 17ths of March occurred in 1521 when Magellan discovered the Philippines, in 1845 when Stephen Perry of London patented the rubber band, and in 1868 when the first postage stamp cancelling machine was patented.

This was the birthday, in 1834, of Gottlieb Daimler. In 1884 it was the date of the first glider flight (by John Montgomery) and in 1898 it saw the first successful lengthy descent by a submarine. A notable ascent on this day was that of Marshall Brooks in 1876, who became the first person to jump higher than six feet.

In 1905, Franklin Delano Roosevelt married Eleanor, and on their first anniversary Theodore Roosevelt became the first person to use the word 'muckrake'. This was also the date of the death in 1992 of Grace Stafford, the voice of Woody Woodpecker.

---

18 March

....

Good day for: *fat women*
Bad day for: *scarecrows*
Beware of: *nightmares*

On this day in 1977 Hassan Abdullah, 41, was reported to be recovering in hospital in Malaysia after his wife had severed his penis while he was asleep. He said that he would not be pressing charges against her, because he accepted her explanation that she had done it accidentally, in her sleep, while she dreamt that she was strangling him.

Invention of the day: the gun-firing scarecrow (US patent 1056602), awarded on 18 March 1913 to John Steinocher of West Texas 'for scaring off birds, animals and such like as tend to prey upon or devastate crops, stock or like property'.

Briton of the day: Prince Philip of Greece, who was naturalised British on this day in 1947.

Memorable event of the day: Britain's first National Fat Women's Conference, held on this day in 1989.

Death of the day: Ivan the Terrible in 1584.

---

19 March

Feast day of St Joseph, patron saint of fathers and carpenters

Good food: *a cup of tea*
Bad food: *sauerkraut*
Lucky form of transport: *lift*

In 1928 on this day, the Industrial Fatigue Research Board said that a cup of tea aids efficiency and curbs industrial discontent. Another aid to efficiency was first marketed three years later when Alka-Seltzer reached the shops in the United States.

This was the day in 721 BC, according to Ptolemy, when the Babylonians were the first to record their observation of an eclipse. It was also the day in 1997 when Singapore officially announced that the number of people convicted of urinating in lifts had dropped from 40 in 1995 to 14 in 1996, thanks to the deterrent effect of an improved urine-detecting device.

Wyatt Earp was born on this day in 1848, while 1996 recorded the tragic death of Julianna Farkas, an 80-year-old Hungarian who drowned in a barrel of sauerkraut in the town of Eles after falling in while trying to spoon more out of the bottom.

20 March

Luck office essential: *duplicator*
Lucky animal: *elephant*
Propitious profession: *singer*

On this day in 1780, James Watt began manufacturing the duplicator. He had invented it to cope with the increased paperwork generated in his office by his invention of the steam engine.

This has not historically been a good day for criminals: in 1806 the foundations were laid for Dartmoor Prison—originally intended to house French prisoners of war—and in 1809 this day saw the execution at York of Mary Bateman. Her body was taken to Leeds Infirmary where 2,500 people paid threepence each to see it. The body was later dissected and the skin tanned and distributed among the crowd.

The Italian tenor Beniamino Gigli and the English songstress Dame Vera Lynn share this birthday, in 1890 and 1917 respectively; but the greatest happiness on this day was reserved for two elephants in Antwerp Zoo who learnt, on 20 March 1997, that solar panels were to be installed to heat 2,000 litres of water each day to give them warm showers.

21 March

Lucky feature: *bare mountains*
Unlucky practices: *vomiting, womanising, nappy-washing*
Favourite music: *Bach cello suites*

This was the birthday in 1685 of Johann Sebastian Bach, and in 1914 of one of the greatest performers of his cello suites, Paul Tortelier. Another composer to have been born on this day was Modeste Mussorgsky, who wrote 'Night on a Bare Mountain'.

In 1923 on this day, French scientists declared that smoking is beneficial to one's health.

More recent 21 March events include:

1989: Bob Hawke, the Australian prime minister, cried on television as he confessed adultery, renounced womanising and thanked his wife for her understanding.
1997: Marikina city council in the Philippines banned vomiting in public, except when linked to sickness or eating rotten food.

Quote of the day: 'Our culture and tradition have a clear division of labour. There are certain household chores that just cannot be done by men'—Governor Welshman Mabhena of Zambia, on 21 March 1996, warning husbands against washing nappies or cooking.

22 March

Earliest date on which Easter may fall

Lucky animal: *black sheep*
Lucky handicap: *dumbness*
Propitious art form: *the musical*

This is the birthday of two of the greatest names in the modern stage musical: Stephen Sondheim (1930) and Andrew Lloyd Webber (1948). With those two hogging all the sound waves, it is little surprise that Marcel Marceau, who was born on the same day in 1923, has preferred to remain silent. The earliest musical connection of the day, however, dates back to 1774 with the publication of *Tom Thumb's Song Book* by Mrs Mary Cooper, including the first appearance of 'Baa, baa, black sheep'.

Water traditionally makes poor progress today, with the US side of the Niagara Falls running dry in 1903 and the Grand Coulee Dam on the Columbia River going into operation in 1941. If your water needs thickening, try cornstarch, invented by Orlando Jones on this day in 1841.

Musical quote of the day: 'Debussy's music is the dreariest kind of rubbish'—*New York Post*, 22 March 1907.

23 March

World Meteorological Day

Good day to: *telephone the president*
Bad day to: *be elected Pope*
Lucky food: *bananas on toast with chicken wings*

This was the day in 1923 of the publication of the song 'Yes, We Have No Bananas', of which the tune was alleged to have been stolen from the Hallelujah Chorus. Two years later, on 23 March 1925, the state of Tennessee banned the teaching of Charles Darwin's Theory of Evolution.

Stephen II was elected to the papacy on this day in 752, and died two days later. Another sad death was that of Dominic Bellissimo on this day in 1991, who was celebrated as the creator of buffalo chicken wings. Another culinary delight associated with this day is Melba toast—for this was the day in 1901 when Dame Nellie Melba revealed the secret of how to make it.

In 1929 on this day, the first telephone was installed in the White House. And 23 March was the date of birth in 1929 of Roger Bannister, the first to break the four-minute-mile barrier, and in 1921 of Donald Campbell, holder of the world water-speed record.

24 March

Feast day of St Gabriel, patron saint of postmen and telephone workers

Unlucky profession: *queen*
Unlucky theory: *atomic fusion at room temperature*
Good day for: *Danish murderers*

In 1953 on this day Queen Mary, the widow of King George V, died. This was hardly an original idea, since Queen Elizabeth I had also died on 24 March, in 1603. It was, however, the date of birth of Steve McQueen in 1930.

Among the Englishmen who followed the example of the above queens in dying on this day were the poets Sir Thomas Malory (died 1471) and Henry Wadsworth Longfellow (died 1882). A Frenchman who got in on the act was Jules Verne, who died on 24 March 1905. Lord Montgomery of Alamein also died on this day, in 1976.

Other deathly occurrences today include the only dead heat in the Oxford–Cambridge boat race, in 1877, and the abolition of the death penalty in Denmark in 1911. All in all it was an inauspicious day for Stanley Pons and Martin Fleischmann in 1989 for publishing their controversial paper claiming atomic fusion at room temperature.

25 March

New Year's Day in England from 1155 to 1752; Pecan Day in the USA

According to the sixth-century religious scholar and calendar-maker Dionysius Exiguus, this was the day in AD 31 of the first Easter. It was also calculated—by working one human gestation period back from Christmas—as the date of the Annunciation to the Virgin Mary, which was why Christian Britain adopted it as New Year's Day from 1155 onwards. All of this made it as good a day as any for the Vatican to launch its Internet site in 1997.

Religion scored another triumph on this day in 1811, when Shelley was expelled from Oxford University for refusing to answer questions about a pamphlet he had written entitled *The Necessity of Atheism*.

Less religiously, it was the date of America's first horse-race in 1668, and the day in 1916 when American women were first allowed to attend a boxing match.

Away from earthly matters, this was the date in 1655 of the discovery by Christiaan Huygens of Titan, Saturn's largest moon, and in 1857 of the first photograph, by Frederick Laggenheim, of a solar eclipse.

26 March

Bad day for: *motorists*
Good day for: *minor injuries*
Lucky vegetable: *spinach*

British motorists were hit by a double whammy on this date, with driving tests being introduced on 26 March 1934 and the first parking tickets issued on the same day in 1958.

This is generally a good day for firsts, with Britain's first official cremation taking place at Woking crematorium in 1885, the first daily weather forecast by the BBC in 1923, the first woman broker setting foot on the floor of the Stock Exchange in 1973, and the first free elections in the USSR in 1989.

Most significantly of all, however, it was the day in 1937 when Popeye became the first cartoon character to have a statue erected in his honour—at Crystal City, Texas, as a gesture of thanks from the local spinach-growers.

It is also a day of great medical advances, with the first medicated adhesive plaster patented on this day in 1845 and Jonas Salk announcing the first vaccine against polio in 1953.

27 March

Lucky letter: *X*
Unlucky number: *307*
Even more unlucky number: *574*

Two of the worst disasters of their type occurred on this day. In 1977 the world's worst air crash happened on the runway in Tenerife when two jumbos collided, killing 574 people. The death toll at Vaal Reef gold-mine in South Africa in 1980 was comparatively small at 23, but they were all passengers in a lift-cage that plunged 1.2 miles or nearly two kilometres—probably the most killed in a lift as well as the longest fall.

The courts have a stern record on this day. In 1567, at the judicatory court in Senlis, France, a sow with a black snout was sentenced to death for murdering a baby; and in 1964, ten members of the gang that committed the Great Train Robbery in England were sentenced to a total of 307 years in gaol.

More positively, this was the day in 1914 when doctors in Brussels performed the first successful human blood transfusion.

Notable birthday: Wilhelm Röntgen (1845), discoverer of X-rays.

Notable death: Yuri Gagarin (1968), the first man in space.

28 March

Good day for: *changing your name*
Bad day for: *rowing*
Politically incorrect genre: *cowboy films*

In 1910 on this day, the first seaplane took off from near Marseilles. Unfortunately, it was nowhere near the River Thames exactly two years later, when both the Oxford and Cambridge boats sank in the boat race.

28 March 1868 saw the death of the Earl of Cardigan, leader of the disastrous Charge of the Light Brigade but more fondly remembered for giving his name to a homely woollen garment. An equally monumental disaster was New Zealand's batting against England in Wellington on this date in 1955 when they were all out for 26, the lowest test match total ever.

This was the day in 1930 when the Turkish cities of Constantinople and Angora changed their names to Istanbul and Ankara, and it was the day in 1973 when Marlon Brando refused to accept an Oscar for his performance in *The Godfather*, in protest against Hollywood's portrayal of Native Americans.

29 March

Favourite film: Chariots of Fire
Favourite drink: *Coca-Cola*
Favourite comet: *Halley's*

This was the day in 239 BC when Halley's comet came closest to the sun on its first recorded passage. This might have been taken as an omen for various later happenings on this day, including the funeral of Beethoven in 1827, at which 10,000 mourners were present, the pull-out of US troops from Vietnam in 1973, and the birth of John Major in 1943.

British successes of the day include Queen Victoria opening the Royal Albert Hall in 1871; Sir William Robertson becoming the first man to complete the rise from the rank of private to field marshal in 1920; and the award of Best Film Oscar to *Chariots of Fire* in 1982.

Anyone with a birthday today should toast it in Coca-Cola, which first went on sale on this day in 1886, having been invented by Dr John Pemberton of Atlanta, Georgia. It was marketed as an 'Esteemed Brain Tonic and Intellectual Beverage' and was hailed as a cure for everything from hysteria to the common cold.

---

30 March

Doctor's Day in the USA

Beware of: *uncles*
Lucky profession: *painter*
Bargain of the day: *Alaska*

On this day in 1842, the American surgeon Dr Crawford Long was the first to use ether as an anaesthetic when he removed a cyst from the neck of a student named John Venable. This anniversary is celebrated on Doctors' Day in the United States.

It could also be Erasing Day, since this was the day in 1858 when Hyman Lipman of Philadelphia patented the pencil with a rubber on the end. This would not, however, be a good choice for Uncles' Day, since it was the day in 1939 when William Hitler, speaking in New York, referred to his uncle Adolf as 'a menace'.

Three renowned painters were born on this day: Francisco de Goya in 1746, Vincent Van Gogh in 1853, and Rolf Harris in 1930.

America bought Alaska from Russia on this day in 1867 at the knock-down price of $7.2 million, but the USA had a rather worse day in 1981 when John Hinckley Jr shot and wounded President Reagan.

31 March

....

Good day for: *fathers*
Bad day for: *guitars*
Lucky states: *Oklahoma, virginity*

In 1943 on this day, the Rogers and Hammerstein musical *Oklahoma!* opened, exactly nine years after the birth in 1934 of the actress Shirley Jones, who was to star in the film version of the same show in 1955.

This was also the day in 1901 when Gottlieb Daimler named his newly designed car after his daughter Mercedes, and the day of birth in 1890 of Sir William Lawrence Bragg, who went on to share the Nobel Prize for Physics with his father in 1915. In 1900 on this day, France limited the working day for women and children to 11 hours, and in 1947 the Bishop of London blamed Hollywood for Britain's high divorce rate.

The USA bought the Danish West Indies for $25 million on this day in 1917 and renamed them the Virgin Islands. Exactly 50 years later, on 31 March 1967, Jimi Hendrix burnt his guitar on stage for the first time. Notable birthday: René Descartes (1596), the father of modern philosophy.

---

1 April

Bank holiday in Burma

....

Fine day for: *terror*
Expansive day for: *underwear, nightwear, overwear, hose, shirt armlets, identification bracelets, pocket-books, pram covers and umbrellas*

If you look up 'April fool' in the 1895 edition of *Brewer's Dictionary of Phrase and Fable*, you will find that it is called in France '*poisson d'avril*' (literally, 'April fish'). The entry for *poisson d'avril* tells us that 'the best explanation is a reference to Matthew xxix. 2', but a quick look at the New Testament reveals that Matthew has only 28 chapters—which, as he says, is about as good a demonstration of April-foolery as one could hope for.

1 April was the birthday of Lon Chaney (1883), star of many horror films, and also the birthday of Edgar Wallace (1875), author of *The Terror*.

On 1 April 1946, wartime restrictions were dropped on the use of elastic in the items mentioned above; on 1 April 1990, it became illegal to be within two feet of nude dancers in Salem, Oregon, and in 1995 the ostrich was zero-rated for VAT as a foodstuff, but its feathers still attract the full tax.

2 April

Recommended destination: *United States*
Recommended mode of transport: *sleeping-car*
Lucky animals: *panda and elephant*

In 1513 on this date, Juan Ponce de León became the first European to set foot on the soil of the future United States when he discovered Florida and claimed it for Spain. It was not until the same day in 1873, though, that British trains were fitted with lavatories, and even then only in sleeping-cars.

On 2 April 1962, push-button panda crossings were introduced in London; and on 2 April 1877 a circus performer named Zazel became the first human cannonball when she was fired at Westminster Aquarium. On precisely the same day, the first Easter Egg roll on the lawns of the White House was held.

Notable births: Charlemagne (742), Hans Christian Andersen (1805).

Quote of the day: 'I have only one eye—I have a right to be blind sometimes ... I really do not see the signal!'—Nelson, aboard HMS *Elephant* at the Battle of Copenhagen on 2 April 1801, putting a telescope to his blind eye.

3 April

Lucky drink: *coffee*
Lucky accessory: *hat*
Lucky number: *31,380,197*

This is the feast day of St Pancras of Taormina, who was sent to evangelise Sicily in the first century. He was reputedly very popular, but not enough to avoid being stoned to death by brigands. He should not be confused with St Pancras of Rome, after whom the London railway station is named.

Notable 'twins': Marlon Brando and Doris Day, both born on 3 April 1924. Notable deaths: Johannes Brahms (1897), Graham Greene (1991). Notable inventions: the coffee mill (patented on 3 April 1829 by James Carrington) and the hat-shaping machine (patented on this day in 1866 by R. Eickemeyer and G. Osterheld).

Bob Ford shot Jesse James in the back of the head on this day in 1882 for a $10,000 purse, which would not have bought much of the Duchess of Windsor's jewellery when it fetched £31,380,197 at auction on this day in 1987.

4 April

....

Bad day for: *kings*
Confusing day for: *women's emancipation*
Lucky vice: *cannibalism*

On 4 April 1887, Susanna Salter became the world's first woman mayor when she was elected to the post in Argonia, Kansas. This contrasts surprisingly with the decision of the Massachusetts state legislature on 4 April 1911 to refuse women the right to vote.

On 4 April 1930 the Archbishop of Canterbury approved the free discussion of sex, and exactly four years later the first cat's-eye reflectors were embedded in a road near Bradford.

Deaths on this day include those of Alfonso X of Spain in 1284, of Frederick II of Denmark in 1558, of King Ghazi of Iraq in 1939 and of Carol II of Romania in 1953. It was also the day of Martin Luther King's assassination in Memphis in 1968.

In 1997 on this day, the release was announced of two Cambodian men who had been held in gaol after eating part of a stillborn baby. Prosecutors could find nothing in the Cambodian legal code to prohibit cannibalism.

---

5 April

....

Good day for: *setting a world record*
Resigned day for: *British politicians*
Favourite food: *fish and chips*

This was the probable date of birth of Giovanni Giacomo Casanova in 1725. If correct, it would be appropriate, for this was the day in 1910 when kissing was banned on French railways because it caused delays, and it was also the day in 1989 when Sex Aid was launched in Britain, with people asked to donate 25 pence each time they had sex.

In 1996 on this day, Harry Ramsden's restaurant in Melbourne set a new world record by serving over 12,000 portions of fish and chips. A year later Dick Auer set a world speed record of 246 kph for in-line skates while clinging to a Porsche on a race-track in Germany.

Winston Churchill resigned as British prime minister on this day in 1955, Harold Wilson gave up the same job on the same date in 1976, and Lord Carrington resigned as Foreign Secretary in 1982.

Quote of the day: 'Be sure you show the mob my head. It will be a long time before they see its like again'—Georges Danton, on 5 April 1794, at the guillotine.

6 April

Feast day of St Elfstan

....

Lucky religions: *Christianity (including Mormonism), and Islam*
Lucky number: *27*
Beware of: *handshakes*

St Elfstan (or Elstan) was a cook with the religious community at Abing-
don, trained by St Ethelwold, at whose command he plunged his hand
into boiling water and took it out unscathed. This has no connection
with the decision of the authorities in Rome on 6 April 1928 to ban
handshaking on grounds of hygiene.

This date has powerful associations in three religions: some biblical
scholars maintain that it is the true date in 6 BC of the birth of Jesus
Christ; it is said to be the day in AD 610 when the Koran was first
revealed to Muhammad; and in 1830 it was the day Joseph Smith and
five associates set up the Mormon Church (Church of Jesus Christ of
Latter-day Saints). A later Mormon leader, Brigham Young, chose this
date to marry his 27th and final wife.

It has been a bad day for the UK: an earthquake hit London in 1580
and Pay-As-You-Earn income tax was introduced in 1944.

---

7 April

....

Good day for: *childbirth*
Noisy day for: *worship*
Lucky numbers: *17 and 39*

On 7 April 1853 Queen Victoria used chloroform during the birth of
her eighth child, Prince Leopold, thus ushering in the age of tolerable
childbirth. In 1958 the Church of England gave its moral backing to
family planning, and in 1997 Vietnam's first gay wedding took place.
The one family blackspot relates to 1832, when James Thompson of
Carlisle sold his wife for 20 shillings and a Newfoundland dog.

On this day in 1995, three women were taken to court by the Holy
Cross Church in Greenburg, Pennsylvania, because they were praying
too loudly and raucously, drowning out the choir and frightening
children.

Sporting records of the day: in 1996 Sanath Jayasuriya scored 50 runs
off 17 balls for Sri Lanka against Pakistan, the fastest one-day 50; and
on the same day Poole Town soccer team drew 0–0 with Barnsley to
bring to an end a 39-match run of losses. One more loss would have
earned a *Guinness Book of Records* entry as worst team of all time.

8 April

Good day to: *change your name*
Lucky flight number: *BA1444*
Lucky religion: *Buddhism*

This was the day in 563 BC when, according to tradition, Buddha was born. It was also the day of the death in 1614 of the painter El Greco, whose real name was Domenikos Theotokopoulos, and the birth in 1893 of the actress Mary Pickford, whose real name was Gladys Smith.

On 8 April 1986 the voters of Carmel, California, made Clint Eastwood's day by electing him mayor, and on the same day in 1776 the first fire escape (consisting of a wicker basket on a pulley and chain) was patented.

At 3.12 a.m. on this day in 1997, Shahana Choudhry, a passenger on British Airways flight BA1444 from Dhaka to Heathrow, gave birth to a boy. It later emerged that another boy had been born on precisely the same flight 13 months earlier.

Notable deaths on this day include the ballet dancer Vaslav Nijinsky, who died in London in 1950, and Pablo Picasso who died in France in 1973.

9 April

Unlucky vocation: *monarch*
Take care of: *your head and ears*
Good day for: *art*

This day saw the death of three monarchs: King Edward IV of England in 1483, Queen Isabella II of Spain in 1904, and King Zog of Albania in 1961. According to different reports, the cause of the death of Edward IV was either 'mortification at the treaty of Arras' or 'excessive debauchery'.

In 1667 on this day the first public art exhibition was held in Paris, and coincidentally on the same date in 1838 the National Gallery opened in London.

On 9 April 1747, Lord Lovat had the dubious privilege of being the last person to be judicially beheaded in England; and this was also the day in 1731 when Captain Robert Jenkins had his ear cut off by the Spanish captain Fandino at Havana, an event which was thought by some to have sparked off the War of Jenkins' Ear between Britain and Spain.

Notable French literary birth: Charles Baudelaire (1821).
Notable French literary death: François Rabelais (1553).

10 April

Unlucky pet: *dog*
Lucky fruit: *banana*
Distinguishing feature: *smelly feet*

In 1633 on this day, bananas first went on sale in Britain.

Nothing of great interest then happened on 10 April until 1849, when Walter Hunt of New York patented the safety-pin. In 1950 on this day, the head of the National Hairdressers' Federation in Britain announced that many men had longer hair than their wives, and in 1988 a dog in East Germany died of a heart attack after being startled by a violent scene in a film on television.

In 1996 this day saw a major advance in the battle against terrorism when Epifanio Lambino Jr, the chief of the Philippines Immigration Bureau civil security unit, told customs officers that international terrorists could sometimes be recognised by their calloused hands and smelly feet.

A survey published on this day in 1997 showed that only 7 per cent of truck drivers think of sex, drink, food and a night out while they are driving; 35 per cent think of their families, and 16 per cent think of nothing at all.

11 April

Dangerous sport: *darts*
Lucky fruit: *Banana*
Good day for: *phoning the Pope*

In 1930 on this day, scientists in New York predicted that there would be a man on the moon by the year 2050. Science recovered its dignity, however, on the same date in 1997 when the journal *Nature* reported that researchers had successfully levitated a frog using a magnetic current.

The most notable birth today was that of Popeye the sailor-man, who made his first appearance in a cartoon strip in 1929. Other significant firsts on 11 April include the first pillar-boxes in London in 1855 and the first telephones on the South Pacific island of Tokelau in 1997, which thus became the last country on earth to install a phone system.

On this day in 1939, Glasgow banned the playing of darts in pubs because it was thought too dangerous; in 1980 Dr Canaan Banana became Zimbabwe's first president; and in 1995 Pierre Brassard, a Canadian comic, spoke on the telephone to the Pope for 18 minutes, pretending to be the Canadian prime minister.

12 April

Feast day of St Zeno of Verona

Good day for: *flying*
Unlucky sex: *male*
Confusing day for: *fish*

Little is known of St Zeno, although 93 of his sermons as Bishop of Verona survive. He is usually represented with a fish, but it is unclear whether this is a symbol of baptism or signifies that he was a keen angler.

On this day in 1911 Pierre Prier made the first non-stop flight from London to Paris, taking just under two hours—almost exactly the same time as Yuri Gagarin took to orbit the earth when he became the first to do so exactly 50 years later on 12 April 1961.

In 1997 on this day, Sattambiye Sriyaratne, a 36-year-old Sri Lankan, was reported to have been arrested for being a man. He had posed as a woman for three years and even won an award for being his country's best female entrepreneur.

Singers born today include Maria Callas (1923), Tiny Tim (1930), Montserrat Caballé (1933) and David Cassidy (1949).

13 April

Good day for: *tap-dancing to Handel's* Messiah
Lucky comet: *Halley's*
Favourite game: *'Scrabble'*

Records indicate that in the year 837 on this day people had the best ever view of Halley's comet.

In 1742 Handel's *Messiah* received its first performance in Dublin, which meant that for exactly 66 years nobody could tap-dance to the Hallelujah Chorus, because William Henry Lane did not perfect the art of tap-dance until 13 April 1808.

The first elephant in America arrived on this day in 1796 from Bengal. London Zoo, however, fought back by offering a home to a 100-year-old tortoise on the same date in 1928.

Births today include one US president: Thomas Jefferson in 1743; one UK prime minister: Lord North in 1732; and the inventor of 'Scrabble': Alfred Butts, in 1899.

On this day in 1959, the Vatican forbade Roman Catholics to vote for Communists, and in 1963 Sidney Poitier became the first black actor to win an Oscar.

14 April

Water Festival in Burma

Lucky colour: *pink*
Unlucky state: *bachelorhood*
Beware of: *icebergs*

On 14 April 1934 Mussolini increased the tax on bachelors by 50 per cent, and on the same day in 1996 Daihatsu became the first car-maker in the UK to put advertising stickers on condom machines.

It's a good day for inventions, with videotape first demonstrated on this day in 1956 and the cordless telephone introduced into Britain in 1983. In 1989, the fight against crime took a step forward when police in Huddersfield announced that research had shown that putting violent prisoners in pink cells had a calming effect.

On this day in 1901, actors were arrested at the Academy of Music in New York for wearing costumes on a Sunday, and in 1912 the *Titanic* struck an iceberg and sank the following day.

Quote of the day: 'Telescopium multis ostendi (lubet hoc uti nomine a meo principe reperto)'—the first recorded reference to a 'telescope', by Prince Federico Cesi, head of the Italian Academy, on 14 April 1611.

15 April

New Year's Day in Bangladesh

Your favourite food: *hamburger*
Your lucky direction: *backwards*
Your lucky language: *English*

In 1755 on this day Samuel Johnson published his *Dictionary of the English Language,* and exactly 200 years later, on 15 April 1955, Ray Kroc found the McDonald's hamburger chain.

This was the birthday of Jeffrey Archer in 1940 and of Samantha Fox in 1966, though probably neither ever received as many birthday presents as did Kim Il Sung, the president of North Korea, when he was sent an estimated 43,000 on his 76th birthday on this day in 1988. This was also the day in 1865 when John Wilkes Booth shot and killed Abraham Lincoln and the day in 1931 when the first organised walk backwards across America began.

On 15 April 1901 the city of Coventry witnessed the first use of a motorised hearse at a funeral, and in 1942 the British government, as a wartime austerity measure, banned embroidery on women's night attire and underwear.

16 April
Militiamen's Day in Cuba

Convenient day to buy: *postage stamps*
Cardinal virtue: *humour*
Lucky colour: *pink*

Two of the most individual of twentieth-century humorists were born on this day: Charlie Chaplin in 1889 and Spike Milligan in 1918. It is also the birthday of the occasionally very humorous Peter Ustinov (1921) and Kingsley Amis (1922), and of the musically witty Henry Mancini (1924) who wrote, among many hits, the *Pink Panther* theme tune.

This was the day in 1705 when Queen Anne visited Trinity College, Cambridge, and knighted Isaac Newton, and, no less momentously, the day in 1922 when Annie Oakley set a women's record by shooting 100 consecutive clay targets. No great feat of invention appears to have happened on this day, unless you include the world's first books of postage stamps which were issued in the USA on this day in 1900.

On 16 April 1997, a survey revealed that 84 per cent of Church of England bishops could name at least one of the Spice Girls.

17 April

Auspicious vocation: *mugger*
Lucky nationality: *Russian*
Bad day for: *watching football*

This was the date of birth in 1480 of that high-class murderess Lucrezia Borgia. In view of this, it was a good date to choose for the first muggers' conference in Bangladesh in 1996, which ended with the title of Master Hijacker being conferred on Mohammed Rippon for his record 21 muggings in two hours.

Other births today include two of the greatest Russians of the Cold War period: Nikita Khrushchev (1894), who was the most powerful man in the USSR from 1953 until 1964; and Mikhail Botvinnik (1911), the first Soviet world chess champion.

It's a fairly accident-prone date, with over 100,000 drowned in the Dutch town of Dort in 1421 when the sea broke through dykes, while in 1996 in Brazzaville in the People's Republic of the Congo, 11 soccer fans were killed by lightning as they watched a match while perched in the branches of a tree.

This was also the day in 1932 when Ethiopia abolished slavery.

18 April

Beware of: *earthquakes*
Good day for: *mad poets and tenors*
Unlucky animal: *pig*

On this day in 1499 in a commune near Chartres, France, a pig was found guilty of the murder of an infant and sentenced to be hanged. The pig's owners were fined eight francs.

In the early hours of the morning of 18 April 1906, the first rumblings of the San Francisco earthquake were felt. It killed over 450 people and destroyed about 28,000 buildings. One who was in San Francisco and lived to tell the tale was the operatic tenor Enrico Caruso who vowed never to visit the city again. Another tenor who can remember 18 April with relief is José Carreras, who gave a recital at Covent Garden on this day in 1989, his first for three years because he had been suffering from leukaemia.

The Boy Scouts launched their first 'bob-a-job week' on this day in 1949, when they would offer to do chores for a 'bob' (one shilling, or five new pence)—twenty chores would thus earn a pound. And this was the day in 1958 when the poet Ezra Pound was released after 13 years in a mental asylum.

19 April

Recommended profession: *actress*
Dubious profession: *lewd actress*
Rejected composer: *Beethoven*

Shirley Temple's first film was released on this day in 1934, exactly one year after the birth of Jayne Mansfield. And on the same date in 1956, the actress Grace Kelly became a princess when she married Prince Rainier of Monaco. The first association of an actress with this date, however, was less salubrious—it was the day in 1926 when Mae West was convicted of indecent behaviour in the production of *Sex* on Broadway. She was sentenced to 10 days in gaol and a $500 fine. This was also the day in 1948 when Paul Raymond's 'Festival of Erotica' opened in London's Soho.

Other achievements on this day by women include Amye Everard in 1637 becoming the first Englishwoman to be granted a patent (for her tincture of saffron and essence of roses), and Kiki Haakonson's victory in the first Miss World Competition in 1951.

On 19 April 1988, Western pop music was permitted on Chinese radio and television—but the song 'Roll Over Beethoven' was banned.

20 April

Lucky literary genre: *detective story*
Inadvisable behaviour: *having sex at a baseball match*
Beware of: *hailstones*

Napoleon III and Adolf Hitler were both born on this day—in 1808 and 1889 respectively. Two years to the day before the second of these two events, the first ever motor-race was organised in Paris. It was won by Georges Bouton in a four-seater quadricycle. He was the only entrant. Exactly 100 years later, on 20 April 1987, Fukashi Kazami of Japan became the first person to reach the North Pole on a motor-cycle.

While tornadoes killed 219 people in Alabama and Mississippi on this day in 1920, that was not as high a toll as the damage done by a hailstorm in Moradabad, India, on the same day in 1888 when 246 were reported to have died.

On 20 April 1996, a couple were convicted in Los Angeles of 'engaging in a sexual act' during a baseball match at Dodger Stadium. They were sentenced to compulsory attendance at AIDS education classes, and to buy 50 baseball tickets each for donation to charity.

21 April

Your favourite food: *horsemeat*
Your lucky language: *American*
Your unlucky profession: *economist*

According to the Roman historian Varro, this was the date in 753 BC when Romulus founded Rome. It is also the first date mentioned, in the year 1600, in James Clavell's novel *Shogun*. Clavell might never have been able to write this novel had Noah Webster not published his *American Dictionary of the English Language* on this day in 1828, but it's not entirely a good day for American literature, since it saw the death of Mark Twain in 1910.

Another notable death on this day was that of the First World War air ace, the Red Baron, Manfred von Richthofen, in 1918—which by an odd coincidence was precisely the same day that the Ministry of Provisions in France encouraged the eating of horsemeat.

Two more who died today were the highly influential economist John Maynard Keynes in 1946 and, in 1952, Sir Stafford Cripps, British statesman, economist and Chancellor of the Exchequer.

22 April

Bad day for: *going roller-skating*
Good day for: *revolutionaries*
Unlucky meal: *gruel*

This day in 1760 saw the first recorded appearance of roller-skates. A Belgian, Joseph Mervin, wore them at a party in Carlisle House, London, while playing the violin. Unfortunately he crashed into a mirror, injuring himself and causing £500-worth of damage.

Vladimir Ilich Ulyanov, better known as Lenin, was born on this day in 1870, and 22 April 1881 saw the birth of Alexander Kerensky, who briefly became leader of Russia after the 1917 revolution.

In 1955 on this day, the US Congress ordered that all coins should bear the words 'In God We Trust', and on the same day in 1983 the British £1 coin came into circulation.

Recent notable events: in 1995 Saudi Arabia held its first beauty competition for camels, an event called 'Miss Dromedary' and held in the town of Umm Raqiba; in 1996, Zhao Jun of Sichuan province, China, died from a burst intestine as he was eating his eighth bowl of gruel in an attempt to win a bet for a packet of cigarettes.

23 April

Peppercorn Day in Bermuda

Good day for: *minor sports*
Bad day for: *unsafe sex*
Terrible day for: *literature*

This was the day in 1564 when William Shakespeare was born—which would have made it a good day for literature had he not died on 23 April 1616, when Miguel de Cervantes, creator of Don Quixote, also died. William Wordsworth died on 23 April 1850, and Rupert Brooke on 23 April 1915.

On this day in 1977, the Czechoslovakian chess grandmaster Vlastimil Hort set a world record by playing 201 games simultaneously. On the very same day, another world record was broken when Dr Allen Bussey completed 20,302 loops of a yo-yo, losing control of it only ten times.

On 23 April 1348, the highest order of English chivalry, the order of the Garter, was founded; on the same day in 1923 Stalin officially opened the Moscow Underground; and in 1984 the discovery of the AIDS virus was announced.

24 April
Armenian Martyrs' Day

Lucky profession: *singer/actress*
Unlucky profession: *cosmonaut*
Favourite drink: *soda*

Shirley MacLaine (1934), Barbra Streisand (1942) and Paula Yates (1960) were all born on this day. They could all have celebrated their birthdays by singing the Marseillaise, which was composed on the very same day in 1792.

The first report of the founding of the Ku Klux Klan appeared on 24 April 1867 and exactly 100 years later Vladimir Komarov became the first cosmonaut to die in space when the Russian ship Soyuz 1 malfunctioned.

Another man to have died on this day was Daniel Defoe, author of *Robinson Crusoe*, in 1731.

Notable events: in 1833 a patent was granted for the first soda fountain; in 1953 Queen Elizabeth II knighted Winston Churchill; and in 1997, Australia launched its first birth control programme for koalas.

25 April
Latest date on which Easter may fall

Recommended profession: *king*
Lucky form of transport: *submarine*
Unlucky animal: *dove*

Two kings were born today: Louis IX of France (1214) and Edward II of England (1284), and to confirm what a good day it is for kingship it was also the birthday of Oliver Cromwell (1599), who became Lord Protector of England, and of Gladys Presley (1912) who became the mother of The King.

On this day in 1989 Ilona Staller, a former stripper turned Italian MP, released a white dove to mark the departure of Soviet troops from Hungary. The dove, however, did not understand what it was meant to do. It sat rather bemused in the middle of the road and was run over by the first tank.

On this day in 1792 Nicholas Peletier became the first man to be guillotined in France, and in 1960 the nuclear submarine *Triton* completed the first circumnavigation of the globe under water.

Invention of the day: the thimble, patented on 25 April 1684.

26 April

Lucky planet: *Saturn*
Lucky animal: *pig*
Beware of: *nuclear power*

Two great philosophers shared this birthday: David Hume in 1711 and Ludwig Wittgenstein in 1889. Less philosophically, this was also the date of the deaths of the great strip-tease artiste Gypsy Rose Lee in 1970 and of the comedienne Lucille Ball in 1989.

Significant events of the day include the following:

1514: Copernicus made his first observations of Saturn.
1895: Oscar Wilde's trial on a charge of homosexuality took place.
1921: the first police on motor-cycles went on duty in London.
1956: the Archbishop of Canterbury declared that Premium Bonds 'debase the nation's spiritual currency'.
1989: Porky's Revenge, the favourite, won the first annual pig-race at Naas in County Kildare, Ireland.
1986: the world's worst nuclear disaster occurred at Chernobyl in the Ukraine.

27 April

Independence Day in Togo and Sierra Leone

Auspicious profession: *psychoanalyst*
Unlucky city: *Venice*
Lucky bird: *woodpecker*

Two men who made a great impact on the twentieth century died on this day: in 1957 Mario A. Gianini, inventor of the maraschino cherry, and two years later Gordon Armstrong, inventor of the incubator for premature babies. Another significant death on this day was that of the navigator Ferdinand Magellan, killed by natives in the Philippines in 1521.

A significant birth on this day was that of Walter Lantz in 1900, the animator who created the cartoon character Woody Woodpecker.

Other significant events include the première in 1749 of Handel's *Music for the Royal Fireworks* (though the performance was unfortunately halted because of fire), the opening in Salzburg of the First International Congress of Psychoanalysis in 1908, the legalisation of abortion in Britain in 1968, and the excommunication in 1508 by Pope Julius II of the entire state of Venice.

28 April

Good day for: *a mutiny*
Bad day for: *Fascism*
Lucky animal: *toad*

This was the day in 1789 when Fletcher Christian took control of the *Bounty* and cast Captain William Bligh and 17 crew members loyal to him adrift in a small boat. It was also a notable date for another British captain when, in 1770, James Cook landed at Botany Bay, Australia, in his ship *Endeavour*.

On 28 April 1780 the *Morning Post* in London carried the earliest advertisement for an abortion clinic. Despite this, Saddam Hussein was born on this day in 1937.

Benito Mussolini, the Italian Fascist leader, had a busy time on 28 April 1945, being captured, tried and shot all within the 24 hours.

On this day in 1987, a toad tunnel under a busy road at Henley-on-Thames in Oxfordshire was pronounced a success. In its first six weeks the number of dead toads on the road had been reduced by 95 per cent.

Invention of the day: the air-conditioner, patented in 1914 by W. H. Carrier.

29 April

Good day for: *music*
Bad day for: *buttons*
Lucky title: *Duke*

In 1818, this was the day of birth of Alexander II, the Russian tsar who emancipated the serfs.

The Duke of Wellington and Emperor Hirohito of Japan were also born today, in 1769 and 1901 respectively, but the date is more generally associated with musical births: the conductors Sir Thomas Beecham (1879) and Sir Malcolm Sargent (1895), and the composer, bandleader and pianist Duke Ellington (1899).

This is also a significant day for innovation: the earliest-known horoscope was devoted to a person born on this date in 410 BC; the zip fastener was patented by Gideon Sundback of Sweden in 1913; in 1930, it became possible to telephone Australia from England; in 1935, Percy Shaw's invention of cat's-eye road reflectors began to be inserted systematically into British roads; and in 1937, Wallace Hume Carothers, who had patented nylon two months earlier, committed suicide.

30 April

Walpurgisnacht in Germany

....

Good day for: *executions*
Lucky country: *United States*
Sport of the day: *table-tennis*

This was the date of three momentous events in the history of the USA: in 1789 George Washington was inaugurated as the first president; in 1803 the country more than doubled in size with the purchase of Louisiana and New Orleans from the French; and in 1900 the republic of Hawaii ceded itself to the United States.

In Britain, this day has provided good work for executions. On 30 April 1650 the Halifax gibbet was used for the last time for the hanging of two thieves, and in 1820 the Cato Street conspirators were hanged, then beheaded.

In 1901 on this day James Gibb launched his new invention, a game he called 'ping-pong'. Other notable firsts today include the first mention of the game billiards, in the *New England Courant* in 1722, and the first practical typewriter, made in Italy by Pelegrini Turri in 1808.

---

1 May

Vappu Day in Finland; Lei Day in Hawaii

....

Good day for: *culture*
Bad day for: *dirt*
Hero of the day: *Batman*

A wide variety of events of high cultural significance have occurred on this day: in 1751, the first cricket match in America was played; in 1786, Mozart's *Marriage of Figaro* had its first performance in Vienna; in 1869, the *Folies Bergère* opened in Paris; in 1939 Batman first appeared, in issue number 17 of *Detective Comics*; and in 1941, Orson Welles' film *Citizen Kane* had its première in New York.

Death of the day: in 1907 Neil Brodie, who was said to have been Canada's dirtiest man, only bathing when ordered by law to do so.

Record of the day: in 1997, Terry Burrows broke the world window-cleaning record, completing three 45-inch square windows in 18.46 seconds.

Most significant anniversary: 1 May 1927—the first cooked meals on a scheduled flight, on Imperial Airways, from London to Paris.

2 May

International Day of Idleness

Good day for: *lying about your birthday*
Bad day for: *obesity*
Unlucky day for: *the Royal Air Force*

When the Association of Free Wanderers of Mar del Plata organised the world's first international tramps' convention in Argentina in 1995, they declared 2 May to be the International Day of Idleness—to counteract 1 May, Labour Day.

Fib of the day: Bing Crosby claimed that his date of birth was 2 May 1904 when he had in fact been born on 3 May 1903. A genuine birth on this day was that in 1892 of the German First World War flying ace, Manfred von Richthofen, also known as the Red Baron.

Scoop of the day: the *Inverness Courier*, on 2 May 1933, reported the sighting of a 'Strange Spectacle on Loch Ness'.

Quote of the day: 'How can a flabby air hostess be of any real help in case of emergency'—a spokesperson for Air India on 2 May 1996, when they grounded 41 cabin crew because they were considered to be overweight.

3 May

Good day for: *a swim*
Bad day for: *busy church-goers in Massachusetts*
Luck profession: *judge*

Birth of the day: Niccolò Machiavelli (1469).

Death of the day: Monsieur Le Pique (1808), killed above Paris in the first ever duel to be conducted from hot-air balloons.

Swim of the day: Lord Byron in 1810 swam the Hellespont in one hour and 10 minutes, to emulate the feat of the legendary Greek Leander, who swam it every evening to be with his lover Hero.

Discovery of the day: Jamaica, sighted by Columbus on this day in 1494—he named it 'St Iago'.

Ruling of the day: in 1675 a law was passed in Massachusetts requiring church doors to be locked during a service. This was thought necessary because too many people had been walking out of churches during long sermons.

Pay rise of the day: in 1949, British High Court judges were given their first pay increase since 1872.

Painting of the day: Goya's *Executions of the 3rd of May*.

4 May
Feast day of St Florian, patron saint of firemen

Lucky mode of transport: *escalator*
Good day for: *art-loving pigeons*
Innovative day for: *women*

This was the day in 1973 when female nudity first appeared on network television in the USA. Six years later to the day, Margaret Thatcher became the British prime minister. This was by no means the worst 4 May for Britain: in 1926 the General Strike began.

It was the fictional day in 1891 when Sherlock Holmes and Professor Moriarty tumbled, supposedly to their deaths, off the Reichenbach Falls. It was also the actual day in 1935 when the world's longest escalator opened, at Leicester Square tube station.

The folding umbrella was patented in Paris on this day in 1715, and in 1995 it was reported that Japanese psychologists had trained pigeons to distinguish between works by Picasso and Monet. But they could not tell a Cézanne from a Renoir.

Disaster of the day: nine worshippers in Kinshasa were trampled to death in 1980 when they were trying to see the Pope.

5 May

Good day for: *being hanged*
Bad day for: *vagrants and sturdy beggars*
Beware of: *the end of the world*

This is the Cinco de Mayo (5 May) holiday in Mexico, celebrating the Battle of Pueblo in 1862. It could also be celebrating the world's first train robbery, which took place near North Bend, Ohio, on the same date in 1865.

Generally this is a day associated more with punishment than with crime. In 1713 a whipping-post was set up at Butter Cross, Doncaster, for 'vagrants and sturdy beggars', and in 1760 the hangman's drop was first used, for the execution of Earl Ferrers at Tyburn. Before that, victims of hanging were left to strangle; the drop killed cleanly by breaking the neck.

Some millennial doom-mongers pick this as the likely moment for the end of the world in 2000, because it is on this day that the Sun, Mercury, Venus, Mars, Jupiter, Saturn and the Moon will be in conjunction.

On 5 July 1988, the Japanese transmitted the first live television pictures from the summit of Mount Everest.

6 May

Good day for: *a bargain*
Bad day for: *marriage*
Lucky art form: *cinema*

This was the day in 1626 when a Dutch official named Peter Minuit bought Manhattan island from the Native Americans for 60 guilders-worth ($24) of knives, beads and cloth.

Rudolph Valentino (1895), Orson Welles (1915) and Stewart Granger (1913) were all born on this date, as were also Maximilien Robespierre (1758) and Sigmund Freud (1856).

In 1950, this was the day of Elizabeth Taylor's first marriage (to Conrad Hilton Jr), and in 1960 Princess Margaret married Anthony Armstrong-Jones. It was also the day in 1890 when the Mormon Church renounced polygamy.

Achievements of the day: in 1851, Dr John Gorrie patented a 'refrigeration machine'; in 1954 Roger Bannister broke the four-minute-mile record. Strike of the day: 1996, when Venetian gondoliers stopped serenading customers when told that it made them freelance musicians, and thus liable to contribute to a state pension fund.

7 May

Good day for: *sex*
Lucky art: *classical music*
Lucky science: *genetics*

This was not only the birthday of Johannes Brahms (1833) and Peter Ilich Tchaikovsky (1840), but it was the day in 1824 of the first performance of Beethoven's 'Choral Symphony'.

It was a good day in 1980 for Paul Geidel, who was freed from Fishkill Correctional Facility in Beacon, New York, after serving a record 68 years and 8 months.

On 7 May 1988 the first gathering was held in Boston, Massachusetts, of people who claim to have been abducted in spaceships. Three years later, geneticists at Johns Hopkins University were given permission to clone Abraham Lincoln's genes from bloodstains, bones and hair.

In 1934 on this day the world's largest pearl, weighing 6.4 kilograms, was found in the seas around the Philippines, and in 1953 a record 537-kilogram swordfish was caught in Chile.

The best news of all, however, came in 1996 when medical researchers at Harvard concluded that sexual activity is unlikely to lead to a heart attack.

8 May

....

Good day for: *animals, especially sharks*
Blissful state: *ignorance*
Beware of: *hailstones*

This is the birthday of two men who have done a good deal to increase our awareness of animals, and of one with a bestial name: the naturalist Sir David Attenborough (1926), the author of *Jaws*, Peter Benchley (1940); and the historian, and author of *The Decline and Fall of the Roman Empire*, Edward Gibbon (1737).

The most significant event of the day occurred in 1886 when John Styth Pemberton perfected the syrup for making Coca-Cola.

Other major events:

1784: the first recorded instance in the United States of people being killed by hailstones occurred in Winnsboro, South Carolina.
1866: Australian Rules football was invented.
1906: British member of parliament Sir W. Anson described the Education Bill as a 'tyrannical imposition of knowledge'.
1921: Sweden abolished capital punishment.
1933: the gas chamber was first used to carry out a death sentence in the USA.

---

9 May

....

Lucky organ: *eye*
Bad day for: *motorists*
Lucky drink: *draught beer*

This was the day in 1969 when the Vatican dropped St Christopher, patron saint of wayfarers and motorists, from the liturgical calendar.

This has been a good day for British innovation: in 1896 the first Horseless Carriage Show, at the Imperial Institute in London, displayed ten vehicles for the motor trade; in 1938 Scotland Yard announced its intention to use police dogs; and in 1949 Britain's first launderette opened. Most significant of all: this was the day in 1785 when Joseph Bramah received a British patent for the beer-pump handle.

On this day in 1924 the YWCA in America advised women to dress strikingly if they wanted to succeed, and in 1944 the first eye bank opened— oddly enough at the Ear, Nose and Throat Hospital in New York.

On 9 May 1995 researchers in Michigan revealed that Americans aged 9 to 12 gossip an average of 18 times an hour, and on 9 May 1996 a board game called 'How to Make Children' was launched in Finland to interest teenage boys in the reproductive side of sex.

---

10 May

Good day for: *mothers*
Lucky vegetable: *asparagus*
Lucky TV series: Rawhide

Not only was this the date of the first Mothers' Day, which was celebrated in Philadelphia in 1907, but in 1937 it saw the first frozen food
in Britain, Smedley's asparagus, going on sale; and it was the birthday,
in 1850, of Sir Thomas Lipton who did so much for tea.

Other birthdays today include John Wilkes Booth (1838) who shot
President Lincoln, Fred Astaire (1899), Sid Vicious (1957) of the Sex
Pistols, Dimitri Tiomkin (1899) who wrote the theme music for the
film *High Noon* and the TV series *Rawhide*, and Dennis Thatcher (1915),
husband of Margaret.

On 10 May 1811 paper money became legal tender in Britain, in 1886
the FA Council approved the awarding of football caps; and in 1967
compulsory breath tests were introduced into Britain by the Road Safety
Bill.

Accident of the day: in 1863, General T. J. 'Stonewall' Jackson died
as a result of wounds sustained when he was shot by his own troops.

11 May

Good day for: *celebrating Christmas*
Unusual relative: *Siamese twin*
Favourite dance: *waltz*

Chang and Eng Bunker, the inseparable pair whose place of birth gave
us the term 'Siamese twins', were born on 11 May 1811; and on 11 May
1939 Siam changed its name to Thailand.

This has been a good day for American innovation: in 1751 Pennsylvania Hospital, the first hospital in the USA, was founded; in 1752 the
country's first fire insurance policy was issued; in 1850, work began on
the first brick building in San Francisco; and in 1947 in Ohio, B. F.
Goodrich manufactured the first tubeless tyre.

This was the day in 1682 when the General Court of Massachusetts
repealed a law that had been passed two years earlier forbidding the
celebration of Christmas.

11 May 1812 was the last time a British prime minister was assassinated: Spencer Perceval was shot by John Bellingham. On the very same
day, the waltz was introduced into Britain and immediately condemned
as immoral.

12 May

Feast day of St Pancras

Good day for: *alcoholics*
Bad day for: *lesbians*
Busy day for: *singers*

St Pancras was a Roman martyr, buried on the Aurelian Way. According to legend, he died in AD 304 at the age of 14.

In 1960 on this day, Elvis Presley appeared on a Frank Sinatra special on television; in 1963, Bob Dylan refused to appear on the Ed Sullivan Show because it was 'too square'; and in 1971 Mick Jagger married Bianca Macias in St Tropez.

Record of the day: in 1986, Fred Markham became the first person to pedal a bicycle at 65 mph on a level course, unaided by wind.

Organisation of the day: Alcoholics Anonymous, founded by William Wilson of Ohio on 12 May 1935.

Quote of the day: 'Lesbians in the sport hurt women's golf' —a remark attributed to Ben Wright on 12 May 1995 in the *New Journal* of Wilmington, Delaware, where he was also quoted as saying that they were handicapped by having breasts.

13 May

Good day for: *slaves*
Lucky shape: *octagon*
Lucky form of transport: *mechanical digger*

This was the date of birth, in 1914, of the great heavyweight boxing champion Joe Louis. He would probably have disapproved to hear that on 13 May 1967 an octagonal boxing-ring was tested in an experiment to see if it would avoid corner injuries.

This is an important day in the history of the Catholic Church: in 1917, three Portuguese shepherd children saw a vision of the Virgin Mary near the village of Fátima; and in 1981 Mehmet Ali Agca shot and wounded Pope John Paul II in St Peter's Square.

In 1888 on this day Brazil abolished slavery, and in 1997 Hugh Edeleanu set a new record of 22 hours, 10 minutes and 30 seconds for driving from John o'Groats to Land's End in a mechanical digger.

Death of the day: Cyrus Hall McCormick (1884), inventor of the mechanical harvester.

Quote of the day: 'I have nothing to offer but blood, toil, tears and sweat'—Winston Churchill, on 13 May 1940.

14 May
Kamuzu Day in Malawi

....

Good day for: *beggars*
Bad day for: *ladies' stockings*
Lucky cooking ingredient: *garlic*

This is an excellent day in the perennial fight against disease: in 1796 Edward Jenner administered his first smallpox inoculation, and in 1997 research at the University of West Virginia showed that garlic slowed bladder cancer in mice.

It is a day of mixed blessings for women: in 1900 the second modern Olympics began in Paris, the first in which women were allowed to compete; but in 1942, the new season of women's war fashions in the UK included 'bare legs for patriotism'.

This day in 1908 saw the first passenger flight in an aircraft; in 1973 the first space station, Skylab, was launched; and in 1996 an 84-year-old German tourist was banned from his flight home from Brazil because he smelled too bad—he had not washed in 42 days.

In 1997, begging was ruled to be legal in Massachusetts, thus overturning a law that had stood since 1886.

15 May
Feast day of St Dymphna, patron saint of the insane

....

Auspicious profession: *air hostess*
Good day for: *nylon stockings*
Bad day for: *immorality*

On 15 May 1930, Miss Ellen Church of Iowa became the world's first air hostess. Applicants for the job had to be no older than 25, weighing no more than 115lb and no taller than 5ft 4in.

On 15 May 1990 Ms Lindi St Clare, also known as 'Miss Whiplash', lost a 15-year battle against the Inland Revenue in which she had claimed that she should not pay taxes because that would mean the state was living off her immoral earnings.

Other notable events of the day:

1718: the machine-gun was patented by James Puckle.
1987: the first Gay Liberation Society was founded in Munich.
1940: nylon stockings went on sale in New York.
1995: a tie 99.6 metres long and six metres wide was rolled out in honour of King Bhumibol of Thailand to celebrate his 50 years on the throne. It was the longest tie in the world.

16 May

Sport of the day: *women's tennis*
Bad day for: *illegal parking*
Undignified day for: *garbage*

This is the birthday of the gymnast Olga Korbut (1955) and of the tennis-player Gabriela Sabatini (1970), and it was also the day in 1934 when Wimbledon decided to allow women players to wear shorts.

Invention of the day: in 1916, Albert B. Pratt of Vermont patented a combination helmet, automatic pistol (fired by blowing) and cooking utensil.

On this day in 1499 a bull was sentenced to death in France for 'furiously killing' a boy; in 1975 Junko Takei of Japan became the first woman to climb Everest; in 1983 the first wheel-clamps came into operation in London; and in 1988 the US Supreme Court ruled that garbage could be searched without a warrant.

Exchange of the day: James Boswell, on his first meeting with Samuel Johnson, said: 'I do indeed come from Scotland, but I cannot help it.' Johnson replied: 'That, sir, I find, is what a very great many of your countrymen cannot help.'

17 May

Good day to: *go on a package holiday*
Favourite reading: *comics*
Lucky ride: *merry-go-round*

In 1620 on this day, the world's first merry-go-round appeared at a fair in Philippopolis (Plovdiv) in Bulgaria. There were probably few English visitors there, since the first package holiday did not happen until this day in 1861, when Thomas Cook arranged for a party from a working men's club to go from London Bridge to Paris for six days.

In 1890 on this day the first weekly comic, called *Comic Cuts*, began publication in London; in 1943, Wing Commander Guy Gibson led the Dam Busters raid on the Möhne and Eder dams in the Ruhr; and in 1998, the European Convention of Tall People began its annual congress in London.

Perhaps the biggest property ever sold in the UK changed hands on 17 May 1938, when the Marquis of Bute sold half of Cardiff, including some 20,000 houses and 1,000 shops, for £20 million.

Birth of the day: Ayatollah Khomeini (1900).

Death of the day: Paul Dukas (1935), composer of *The Sorcerer's Apprentice*.

18 May

Good day for: *mowing the lawn*
Bad day for: *parents*
Cosy room: *lavatory*

On this day in 1830 Edwin Budding of Stroud, Gloucester, signed an agreement for the manufacture of 'machinery for the purpose of cropping or shearing the vegetable surface of lawns'.

It's a good day for women: in 1920 Oxford University gave equal status to women professors, and in 1953 an American, Jacqueline Cochrane, became the first woman to break the sound barrier.

Law of the day: in 1996, the High Court in Rome ruled that parents must not smack their children even if they think the smack is of educational value.

Two tennis champions were born today: Fred Perry (1909) and Yannick Noah (1960).

Quote of the day: 'Where can you find a country with so many public toilets? And so well maintained, too. British lavatories are not just spotlessly clean, they are cosy'—Anatoly Adamishin, Russian ambassador, on leaving London on 18 May 1997.

19 May

Brave day for: *donkeys*
Sad day for: *tortoises*
Jumpy day for: *frogs*

In 1536 on this day, Anne Boleyn was beheaded. Another woman whose funeral was held today was Mrs Sandra West, who was buried in 1977 in San Antonio, Texas, according to the terms of her will: 'next to my husband, in my lace nightgown . . . in my Ferrari, with the seat slanted comfortably'. To round off a generally miserable day for women, in 1982 Sophia Loren was jailed for tax evasion. More cheeringly, in 1991 Helen Sharman became the first Briton in space.

Beastly matters of the day: in 1928, 51 frogs entered the first Frog Jumping Jubilee at Angel's Camp, California; in 1966, the tortoise said to have been given to the King of Tonga by Captain Cook died; and in 1997 in Canberra, a donkey named Murphy was posthumously awarded the Purple Cross for bravery at Gallipoli in 1915.

Law of the day: in 1910 a court at Westminster decided that taxi-drivers could be prosecuted for asking for tips.

Birth of the day: Ho Chi Minh (1892).

20 May

Oil Nationalisation Day in Iran

....

Good day for: *clones*
Bad day for: *phones*
Lucky comet: *Halley's*

This is a musical day: in 1915 the Russian pianist Sviatoslav Richter was born, and in 1917, the singer Vera Lynn. It's also the date of birth of Napoleon II in 1811, and the day in 1815 when Napoleon Bonaparte entered Paris after his escape from Elba.

On 20 May 1969 John Lennon married Yoko Ono. On this day in 1996, Cambridge University Library banned the use of mobile phones, and in 1997 Dolly the cloned sheep was shorn and her fleece donated to the Cystic Fibrosis Fund.

The end of the world was predicted for this day in 1910, when the earth passed through the tail of Halley's comet. There was a brisk trade in 'comet pills' in the USA, and no one who bought them was damaged by the comet—but neither was anyone else.

Arrest of the day: Guy Trébert in Paris in 1959, the first person apprehended by means of an Identikit picture.

21 May

....

Unlucky car part: *bumper*
Unlucky dances: *foxtrot and tango*
Good day for: *the British in Australia*

This day in 1997 marked a landmark in the history of Australia, when the Human Rights Commission ruled that 'pom' and 'pommie' are no longer terms of racial abuse.

On 21 May 1819 the first bicycles in America, known as 'swift walkers', were seen on the streets of New York City. Another transport innovation came in 1898, when the first motor-car bumper was fitted to a prototype vehicle at the Imperial Wesseldorf wagon factory in Moravia. It set off on a test run to Vienna, but the bumper fell off within the first ten miles. To round off a generally exciting day for transport, this was also the day in 1927 when Charles Lindbergh landed his *Spirit of St Louis* near Paris to complete the first solo aeroplane flight across the Atlantic.

Four years earlier in Paris, the International Congress of Dancing Masters condemned the tango and foxtrot, and in 1979 Elton John was the first Western rock star to perform in the USSR.

22 May

....

Opera of the day: Rigoletto
Good day for: *cartoons*
Bad day for: *beauty*

In 1892 on this day a British dentist, a Dr Sheffield, invented the tooth-paste tube. In 1921 the city of Chicago instituted fines on women with bare arms or short skirts, and exactly eight years later Mussolini banned beauty contests in Italy as immoral. Another ban came in 1959 when the Albanian censors banned a children's book because the plot included a black rabbit marrying a white one. It was a better day for rabbits in 1997 when Bugs Bunny became the first cartoon character to be honoured on an American postage stamp.

Human rights issue of the day: in 1996 a court in Kassel, Germany, ruled that policemen have the right to wear their hair in a plait and cannot be ordered by a superior to remove it.

Cultural event of the day: in 1853 the *Gazette Musicale de Paris* wrote: 'Rigoletto is the weakest work of Verdi. It lacks melody. This opera has hardly any chance of being kept in the repertoire.'

23 May

Feast day of St Euphrosyne of Polotsk

....

Good day for: *getting married under water*
Bad day for: *Nazis*
Unlucky profession: *optician*

St Euphrosyne of Polotsk (died 1173) was a recluse and is not to be confused with St Euphrosyne of Alexandria, who dressed as a man, called herself Smaragdus, and joined a monastery to avoid marriage.

In 1785, the 79-year-old Benjamin Franklin explained that his invention of bifocals made it no longer necessary for him to carry two pairs of glasses with him.

It's a bad day for villains: in 1701 Captain William Kidd was hanged for piracy and murder; in 1934 Bonnie Parker and Clyde Barrow were killed in a police ambush in Louisiana; in 1945 Heinrich Himmler committed suicide, and in 1960 Adolf Eichmann was kidnapped by Israeli agents in Argentina.

On 23 May 1988, Fleming Koch and Nina Tolgard were married on an underwater reef in Mauritius, taking their vows in divers' sign language.

24 May

On his deathbed on this day in 1543 Nicholas Copernicus was brought the first copy of his treatise, *On the Revolutions of the Heavenly Spheres*. For ever after, the earth ceased to be considered the centre of the universe.

Europe began a tradition of musical mockery in 1956 with the first Eurovision Song Contest, won by Switzerland. The Middle East had a cold day in 1988, with the first snow in Damascus for 50 years.

France has had the worst of the day: in 1809 Dartmoor Prison was opened to house French prisoners of war, and in 1920 President Deschanel of France fell out of a train dressed only in his pyjamas.

Quotes of the day: (1) 'What hath God wrought?'—Samuel Morse's first message transmitted in 1844 by telegraph; (2) 'If this is justice, I'm a banana'—Ian Hislop's assessment after Sonia Sutcliffe, the Yorkshire Ripper's wife, was awarded £600,000 damages against *Private Eye* magazine in 1989.

25 May

This was the day in 1995 when Alaskans were first permitted to own an elephant, and in 1850 it was the day Britain caught its first sight of a hippopotamus, on its way to London Zoo. Another British first followed in 1857, when the Oxfordshire Light Infantry became the first regiment to wear khaki (the word is derived either from *karkeerung*, native cloth, or the Urdu *kaki*, dust-coloured).

Jesse Owens had a good day in 1935 when he broke five world records (long jump, 220 yards, 200 metres, 220 yards hurdles, 200 metres hurdles) and equalled a sixth (100 yards), all within an hour.

In 1986 around 7 million Americans took part in 'Hands Across America', forming a line across the country, and in 1995 the first International Symposium on Public Toilets opened in Hong Kong.

Quote of the day: 'History is more or less bunk . . . the only history that is worth a tinker's damn is the history that we make today'—Henry Ford on 25 May 1916.

26 May

Good day for: *gambling*
Bad day for: *being hanged in public*
Recommended profession: *poet*

This was the day in 1887 when it became legal to bet on horses at American race-tracks. Oddly enough, it was the same day in 1978 that the first legal gambling casino opened in Atlantic City.

Today's birthdays include the Russian poet Alexander Pushkin (1799) and the English poet A. E. Housman (1859), while popular culture celebrates Al Jolson (1886) and John Wayne (1907). Other cultural events include the opening in Moscow in 1988 of the musical *Cats*, and the start of a bed-in for world peace by John Lennon and Yoko Ono in room 1742 of the Hotel de la Reine, Montreal, Canada.

It was a momentous day for the Middle East in 1908, when the first major oil strike in the region was made in Persia, and an even more momentous day for Michael Barrett in 1868, when he became the last person to be hanged in public in Britain.

More significantly, perhaps, on 26 May 1946 a patent application was filed in the USA for the H bomb.

27 May

Good day for: *horror*
Bad day for: *mental illness*
Unlucky profession: *witch*

This was the birthday of two of the greatest horror film actors: Vincent Price (1911) and Christopher Lee (1922). Their colleague Peter Cushing just missed making it a triple celebration, having been born a day earlier, on 26 May 1913.

Appropriately enough for horror fans, this was also the day in 1647 when Achsah Young became the first documented case of a woman executed for being a witch. Also, in 1863 in England, Broadmoor was established, the first asylum for the criminally insane. In 1907 bubonic plague broke out in San Francisco on this day, but the city had a happier 27 May in 1937 when the Golden Gate Bridge was dedicated.

Trial of the day: in 1988, a Canadian who had driven 14 miles to his mother's home where he hit her with an iron bar and stabbed her, was acquitted of murder because medical evidence proved that he had done it all while sleepwalking.

28 May

Feast day of St Bernard of Montjoux, patron saint of mountaineers

Good day for: *the birth and death of kings*
Lucky animal: *monkey*
Lucky method of execution: *guillotine*

St Bernard, after whom the dogs were named, was an eleventh-century canon who built rest-homes for weary Alpine travellers.

King John the Fearless of France (born 1371) shares this birthday with King George I of England (1660). The only British king to have died on 28 May was the Duke of Windsor (in 1972), who had been Edward VIII before his abdication. Other great British births on this day include William Pitt the Younger (1759) and Ian Fleming (1908), while France can boast Dr Joseph Ignace Guillotin (1738), whose invention was softened by adding a feminine *e* to his surname.

Sporting anniversaries: on 28 May 1742 England's first indoor swimming-pool opened in London, and in 1891 the first world weight-lifting championships were held at the Café Morico in London's Piccadilly.

In 1959 two American monkeys, Able and Baker, became the first animals to return safely from a trip into space.

29 May

Oak-apple Day in England

Good day for a: *bank holiday*
Bad day for: *the Middle Ages*
Lucky body part: *groin*

This day used to be celebrated in England as both the birthday of Charles II in 1630 and the day in 1660 when he set foot in England to reclaim the throne. Royalists used to mark the day by decorating their homes with oak branches and leaves.

In 1871 this was Britain's first official bank holiday – nothing to do with oaks, this was the day when Whit Monday fell. Another bank holiday has associations with this date, for it was the day in 1942 when Bing Crosby recorded 'White Christmas'.

29 May 1453 was when Constantinople fell to the Turks, an event taken by some historians to mark the end of the Middle Ages.

Sporting events: in 1922, the US Supreme Court declared baseball to be a sport and thus not subject to anti-trust laws, and in 1997 the Babe Ruth Baseball League in Florida changed its rules to enable a girl catcher to play without wearing a groin protector.

30 May

Great day for: *cartoons*
Disastrous day for: *literature*
Garment of the day: *brassière*

Four great writers and one painter died today: Christopher Marlowe (1593), Alexander Pope (1744), Voltaire (1778), Boris Pasternak (1960) and Peter Paul Rubens (1640). To make up for this, however, it was the birthday, in 1908, of Mel Blanc, who was the voice of Bugs Bunny, Daffy Duck and Elmer Fudd, among many other cartoon heroes.

This was also the day in 1848 when William Young patented the ice-cream freezer, and in 1889 when the brassière was invented.

More deaths: in 1431, Joan of Arc was burnt at the stake, and in 1911 Sir William Schwenck Gilbert, who wrote the words to Sullivan's music, drowned in a pond near Harrow while giving swimming lessons to two schoolgirls. He was 74.

Invention of the day: in 1959, the first experimental hovercraft, designed by Christopher Cockerell, was launched at Cowes on the Isle of Wight.

31 May

Inauspicious day to: *launch a ship*
Lucky number: *15,007,003*
Lucky jewellery: *ear-rings*

This was the day in 1678 when Lady Godiva is said to have ridden naked through Coventry as a protest against taxation. It was the day in 1911 when the *Titanic* was launched, though her maiden and final voyage was not until the following year. Another form of transport came to a happier end on this day in 1927: the final Model T Ford rolled off the production line, number 15,007,003 of its type.

On 31 May 1669, bad eyesight forced Samuel Pepys to give up writing his *Diary*; in 1825 the Englishman William James patented a device for scuba-diving; and in 1909, Count Zeppelin set a new record of 37 hours in an airship before he crashed into a pear tree in Stuttgart when landing to refuel.

Human rights victory of the day: in 1988, a court in Norway ruled that a soldier had the right to wear ear-rings on parade.

Births of the day: Prince Rainier III of Monaco (1923), Clint Eastwood (1930), Terry Waite (1939).

1 June

Elfreth's Alley Day (the oldest US street) in Connecticut

Favourite drink: *Scotch*
Lucky hobby: *underwater 'Monopoly'*
Unlucky instrument: *electric guitar*

The earliest written records of Scotch whisky appeared on this day in 1495 in the Exchequer Rolls of Scotland. After this, nothing of great interest happened on 1 June until 1638 when the first earthquake recorded in the United States hit Plymouth, Massachusetts.

Other firsts on this date include Edison's first invention—an electric vote-recording machine—in 1869; the first driving tests were introduced in Britain in 1935; the first television licences in Britain in 1942; and the first seismograph in California in 1898.

The major events of the day include Bob Dylan being booed by purists at the Albert Hall in London in 1966 when he used an electric guitar, and the breaking of the world underwater 'Monopoly' record by five members of a Belgian diving club who played for 30 hours and 15 minutes.

2 June

Seamen's Day in Iceland

Unlucky profession: *weather forecaster*
Unlucky song: *'When the Saints Go Marching In'*
Bad day for: *telling jokes*

This was the date chosen in 1953 for the coronation of Queen Elizabeth II because records showed it to be the most consistently sunny day of the year. It rained.

In 1886 on this day, Grover Cleveland became the first US president to wed during his term of office, and a Central American first was achieved on 2 June 1930 with the first baby to be born on a ship passing through the Panama Canal.

On 2 June 1971, the *Sun* newspaper reported that an elephant named Iris at Twycross Zoo in Leicestershire had been taught to play 'When the Saints Go Marching In' on the mouth-organ. The unluckiest people of the day were two Estonians, Valdo Yahillo and Erkki Kylu, who finished their world record bid of 61 hours of non-stop joke-telling on 2 June 1997 only to find that they had based their performance on an old edition of the *Guinness Book of Records* and that the record was now over 100 hours.

3 June

Buddhist Memorial of Broken Dolls

Animal of the day: *salamander*
Good day for: *sunbathing*
Beware of: *volcanoes*

This is a date of mixed fortunes for the British royal family: on this day in 1865 the future King George V was born, and in 1937 it was the day ex-king Edward VIII married Wallis Simpson. Another significant birth on this day was that of Henry Shrapnel in 1761, who invented and gave his name to the shrapnel shell.

Two memorable deaths, both with Japanese connections, occurred on this day. In 1881, a Japanese giant salamander died in a zoo in the Netherlands at the age of 55—it was the world's oldest known amphibian. In 1991, an eruption of Mt Unzen in Japan claimed the life of the vulcanologist Harry Glicken.

Notable events of the day: in 1946 a Paris fashion show saw the first appearance of the bikini; in 1996 the education ministry in Thailand imposed weight limits on school-bags: 1 kilogram for kindergarten, 2 kilograms for elementary school, 3 kilograms for high school.

4 June

Great day for: *ballooning*
Fine day for: *shopping*
Gay day for: *fruitflies*

On this day in 1783, the Montgolfier brothers launched their first (unmanned) hot-air balloon, and exactly a year later one Madame Thible, watched by the King of Sweden, became the first woman to fly in one. The benefit to humanity of these events, however, can hardly be compared to the appearance in Oklahoma, on 4 June 1937, of the first supermarket trolley, or the production, on this same day in 1070, of the first Roquefort cheese in a cave near Roquefort, France.

4 June 1997 was declared National Pizza Day by the US Congress in celebration of 100 years of pizza-eating in America, while on the same day in 1995 researchers in Washington reported that transplanting a single gene can induce homosexual behaviour in fruitflies.

Disaster of the day: in 1995 an attempt on the world tug-of-war record by 600 scouts in Germany left two dead and 60 injured when the nylon rope suddenly snapped.

5 June

··

Good day for: *lavatories*
Favourite fruit: *banana*
Lucky number: *17,378,581*

According to the ancient Mayan calendar, this was the day, in 8239 BC, of the Creation. More recently, it was the date in 1973 when Britain voted by 17,378,581 votes to 8,470,073 to enter the Common Market.

America also has cause to rejoice today, for it was the appearance of bananas at the International Centennial Exhibition in Philadelphia on this day in 1876 that led to the fruit's great popularity in the USA.

While Tiananmen Square in Beijing is generally associated with 3 and 4 June 1989 when a massacre of students took place, it should not be forgotten that 5 June 1995 was the date of the opening, at the Museum of the Cultural Revolution in Tiananmen Square, of China's first exhibition of lavatories.

Coincidence of the day: in 1939 this was the date of birth of both Margaret Drabble (author of *The Needle's Eye*) and Ken Follet (author of *Eye of the Needle*).

6 June

··

Lucky disability: *deafness*
Lucky housework: *ironing*
Bad day for: *singin' in the rain*

This was the day in 1995 when a deaf bank cashier in Tel Aviv averted a robbery. The robber, with a gun hidden in his bag, whispered: 'Hold-up!' The cashier said: 'Sorry, sir, could you say that again?' He replied, a little louder: 'I said this is a hold-up.' 'Please speak up. I can't hear a word,' she said. And when he realised she was genuinely hard of hearing, he gave up and fled.

Apart from that, this date is notable as the day in 1882 when Henry Seely of New York patented the first electric iron; and as the day in 1914 when, for the first time, an aeroplane disappeared from sight of anyone on land, in a flight from Scotland to Norway. On this day in 1933 the first drive-in movie opened in Camden, New Jersey; in 1988, David Stern of New York blew the world's biggest bubble, 50ft long; and in 1995 a production of *Singin' in the Rain* at the Playhouse Theatre, Edinburgh, had to be halted because of flooding.

Today is also the King's Birthday holiday in Malaysia.

7 June

Good day for: *dates*
Auspicious day for: *foreign travel*
Lucky building: *the Taj Mahal*

In 1502 on this day Pope Gregory XIII was born, but for whom we might not have had the Gregorian calendar on which this book is based. The death of the day was that of Mumtaz Mahal in 1629. Her husband, Shah Jahan of India, had the Taj Mahal built as her tomb.

On this day in 1099 the armies of the First Crusade reached the walls of Jerusalem. It was also the day in 1939 when George VI and Elizabeth became the first King and Queen of Britain to visit the United States, and in 1972 when German Chancellor Willy Brandt visited Israel. On 7 June 1955, General Eisenhower became the first US president to appear on colour television.

On 7 June 1988, a Brazilian dentist fitted a plastic beak to a parrot in a local zoo, enabling it to eat again after its own lower beak had split. And on 7 June 1995, a woman named Ramyanka in India was reported to have chopped off the penis of her alleged lover, Mangu Das, in order to prove her future fidelity to her husband.

8 June

Good day for: *women*
Bad day for: *leaders of men*
Lucky detective: *Sherlock Holmes*

Three major events in the emancipation of women occurred on this day: in 1824 a washing-machine was patented by Noah Cushing of Quebec; in 1847, the working day for British women and children was limited to ten hours; and in 1923, the Matrimonial Clauses Bill allowed women to divorce their husbands for adultery.

This was the day in 1978 when Naomi James of New Zealand became the first woman to sail round the world single-handed; in 1940 when Nancy Sinatra was born; and in 1979 when Michael Wilding, one of Elizabeth Taylor's ex-husbands, died.

It was also the date of death of Muhammad, the prophet and founder of Islam, in 632; of Edward the Black Prince in 1376; and of Andrew Jackson, the seventh president of the USA, in 1845.

Finally, this was a busy day for Sherlock Holmes, marking the start of the *Boscombe Valley Mystery* in 1889 and *The Adventure of the Six Napoleons* in 1900.

9 June

··

Bad day for: *feeding the hungry*
Unlucky day for: *bagpipers*
Beware of: *tooth decay*

On this day Anthony Eden resigned as British prime minister in 1957, and Nero committed suicide in AD 68.

Notable births today include railway pioneer George Stephenson (1781) and songwriter Cole Porter (1891); and Donald Duck, who made his debut in *The Wise Little Hen* on this day in 1934.

In California, on 9 June 1996, Robert Norse Kahn was ordered to serve 59 days in gaol for handing out food to the homeless without a permit—the first conviction in the USA for feeding the hungry; and in Britain on the very same day, the organisers of the Euro 96 football championships included bagpipes on a list of offensive weapons that could not be brought into matches.

Quote of the day: 'Weak teeth are the sign of a strong hand'—a headline in *Komsomolskaya Pravda* on 9 June 1995 above an interview with the veteran Kremlin dentist Alexei Donikov, who revealed that Stalin had only three of his own teeth when he died.

---

10 June

Time Observance Day in Japan (to encourage punctuality)

··

Good day for: *lightning*
Lucky condiment: *mustard*
Lucky letter: *any written in ball-point and sealed in a window envelope*

This is an especially good day for naturalised Britons, being the date of birth in 1921 of the Greek who became the Duke of Edinburgh, and in 1923 of the Czech who became newspaper tycoon Robert Maxwell. It was not a good day for Mickey Mouse in 1988, when he was accused by a US clergyman of snorting coke; a spokesman for CBS, however, insisted he had only been sniffing flowers.

In 1720 on this day, Mrs Clements marketed the first spreadable mustard paste in England; in 1902, H. F. Callahan received a patent for his invention of the window envelope; and in 1943 Laszlo Biro patented his ball-point pen.

It was also the day in 1752 when Benjamin Franklin's kite was struck by lightning in a famous physics experiment, which explains why the same date was chosen in 1932 for the first demonstration, in Pittsfield, Massachusetts, of artificially induced lightning.

---

11 June

Sport of the day: *cricket*
Infestation of the day: *cockroaches*
Plat du jour: hot dog

A number of cricketing records were made on this date: in 1911, Nottinghamshire were all out for 12 against Gloucestershire; in 1952 Denis Compton hit his 100th century; and in 1953 Len Hutton became the first professional to captain England. It has not been such a good day for football, especially in 1995 when three Genoa fans died of heart attacks when their team lost a crucial relegation play-off against Padova on penalties.

On this day in 1939 at a party organised by Franklin D. Roosevelt, King George VI and Queen Elizabeth became the first British monarchs to taste hot dogs.

On 11 June 1997 Mary Esposito of Forest Park, Georgia, won $1,000 and a supply of cockroach-control products as a prize in a contest to find the worst-infested home in the USA. She had an estimated 75,000 cockroaches.

Event of the day: 1872—the last time the stocks were used in Britain.

12 June

Feast day of St John of Sahagún

....

Bad day for: *going over Niagara Falls in a barrel*
Lucky body part: *knee*
Lucky name: *Christophpher* (sic)

St John of Sahagún was a fifteenth-century Spanish friar who denounced oppressive landlords. He is believed to have been poisoned by a woman whose lover he had persuaded to reform.

Birth of the day: British prime minister Anthony Eden (1897).

Death of the day: Charles Stephens (1920), killed when he went over Niagara Falls in a barrel.

Other events of the day: in 1667 Jean-Baptiste Denys, physician to Louis XIV, carried out a successful blood transfusion on a 15-year-old boy using sheep's blood; in 1996 Bavarian doctors performed the world's first knee transplant, and on the same day in Sweden Pia Agergaard won a nine-year battle to be allowed to call her son Christophpher, rather than Christopher or Christoffer.

Anomaly of the day: on 12 June 1965 the Beatles were made MBEs, but it was the Rolling Stones who released 'Satisfaction'.

13 June

Feast day of St Anthony of Padua, patron saint of lovers and the poor

Good day for: *a train journey*
Mixed day for: *attempting suicide*
Beware of: *hailstorms*

In Taiwan on this day in 1995, 38-year-old Huang Chia-yuan, a failed novelist, attacked six cars with a hammer in the hope that their owners would kill him. He had already tried other methods recommended in the *Complete Suicide Book*. Unluckily, as he was being beaten up, he was rescued by the police and taken to hospital with severe bruising.

One who had better luck with his suicide was mad King Ludwig II of Bavaria who drowned himself on this day in 1886, but his psychiatrist Bernhard von Gudden also died trying to save him.

In 1842 on this date, Queen Victoria became the first British monarch to travel by train when she went from Slough to Paddington. It was also the day in 1789 when George Washington became the first US president to taste ice-cream.

Disaster of the day: 22 people killed by hailstones in Siatista, Greece, in 1930.

14 June

Mothers' Day in Afghanistan

Good day for: *school chemistry labs*
Bad day for: *pigs*
Safe day for: *women*

On this day in 1494, the grand mayor of the church and monastery of St Martin de Laon condemned a pig to be hanged and strangled for infanticide. In 1906 on this day, the British parliament passed a bill banning women from dangerous sports after a female parachutist had fallen to her death.

This is an especially good day for people who gave their names to things, being the birthday of Charles Augustin de Coulomb (1736), the physicist who established Coulomb's law, and of Alois Alzheimer (1864), the German neurologist who described what came to be known as Alzheimer's disease. It was also the day in 1847 when Robert Bunsen invented his burner. The most notable creative event of the day, however, was the patenting of sandpaper by Isaac Fischer in 1834.

Quote of the day: 'Britain is great again'—Margaret Thatcher on 14 June 1982 following Argentina's surrender in the Falklands War.

15 June

Feast day of St Vitus, protector of epileptics

Good day for: *Dukes of Burgundy*
Black day for: *princes*
Happy day for: *hookers*

This is the day of birth of Edward the Black Prince (1330), of Philip the Good, Duke of Burgundy (1396), and of Xaviera Hollander (1942) who called her autobiography *The Happy Hooker*.

On this day in 1934, Hitler met Mussolini for the first time, and in 1988 Rabbi Moshe Hirsch asked Yasser Arafat to intervene to close a sex shop in Jerusalem that was selling pornographic videos and inflatable Chinese dolls.

It has been a mixed day for aviation: in 1928, the train the *Flying Scotsman* beat an aircraft in a race from London to Edinburgh; in 1919, Alcock and Brown reached Ireland after the first non-stop transatlantic flight; and the world's first fatal aviation accident happened on this day in 1785, when two French balloonists died.

An even bigger disaster struck Sanriku, Japan, on 15 June 1896, when a tsunami (tidal wave) struck a Shinto festival on the beach, killing an estimated 27,000 people.

16 June

Extraterrestrial day for: *women*
Lucky headgear: *bonnet*
Lucky garment: *swimsuit*

On this day in 1963, Valentina Tereshkova became the first woman in space. The date was already well established as an important one in the history of the women's movement, for it was the day in 1880 when female members of the Salvation Army first wore bonnets, and in 1930 when mixed bathing was first allowed in the Serpentine in London's Hyde Park.

On 16 June 1216 Pope Innocent III died, and on 16 June 1995 Kitty Cat, the richest cat in Oregon, died at the age of 19; twelve years earlier, she had been left a $250,000 mansion by her late owner John Bass.

Other notable events of the day: in 1903 the Pepsi-Cola trade name was registered; in 1948, the first airline hijack took place on a flight from Macao to Hong Kong; in 1978, the game of 'Space Invaders' was first demonstrated. Most notably, 16 June 1904 was the date on which the events in James Joyce's novel *Ulysses* took place.

17 June

Good day for: *going out in the rain*
Bad day for: *being guillotined*
Lucky body part: *kidney*

This was the day in 1823 when the Scottish chemist Charles Macintosh patented the waterproofing method that led to what is now known as the mackintosh. There is no satisfactory explanation of why a *k* was added to the middle of the inventor's name.

It's a doubly important date for human organs: on 17 June 1867, Joseph Lister performed a mastectomy on his sister, in the first operation using carbolic acid as an antiseptic. On the same date in 1950, the world's first kidney transplant was performed in Chicago. A rather cruder form of bodily alteration happened on 17 June 1939, when Eugen Weidmann was the victim of the last public guillotining in France.

Invention of the day: the musical condom, launched in Hungary on 17 June 1996 by Ferenc Kovacs. It plays a tune as it is unrolled, with buyers able to choose from a selection including an old Communist song, 'Arise Ye Worker.'

18 June

Recommended vocation: *insurance salesman*
Lucky colour: *blue*
Dangerous sport: *nude cathedral-climbing*

On 18 June 1583, Richard Martin of London took out the first life insurance policy, paying a premium of £383 to insure the life of one William Gibbons. Apart from having been a good day for insurance salesmen, this has also been auspicious for songwriters, being the birthday of both Sammy Cahn (1913) and Paul McCartney (1942).

Achievement of the day: on 18 June 1995, a naked man climbed 105 feet up Strasbourg Cathedral. After police and firemen had helped him down, they discovered he had fled from a psychiatric unit, to which they returned him.

Discovery of the day: 'the sandcastle effect', identified by researchers at the University of Notre Dame, Indiana, and first published on 18 June 1997, explaining why sandcastles do not collapse after the sand in them has almost totally dried out.

Film of the day: *The Blues Brothers*, starring John Belushi and Dan Aykroyd, had its première on this day in 1980.

19 June

Good day for: *putting on clean underwear*
Bad day for: *drinking, smoking, gambling and joking*
Superlative day for: *fruit*

On this day in 240 BC, Eratosthenes estimated the circumference of the earth with considerable accuracy. More than 2,200 years later, on 19 June 1981, India's Apple satellite was launched, the first to orbit the earth with all three of its axes stable. Oddly enough, on the very same day that Apple was launched the heaviest known orange was exhibited in South Africa, weighing in at 2.5 kilograms.

A survey published on this day in 1995 revealed that 1 per cent of British adult males change their underwear once a week or less; and on the very same day the Shanghai Stock Exchange banned drinking, smoking, gambling, eating snacks, opening canned drinks, sleeping, shouting or 'joking around'.

Other notable 19 June events: in 1910, Fathers' Day was first celebrated in Spokane, Washington; in 1977, Pope Paul VI canonised John Neumann, the USA's first male saint.

20 June

Good day for: *bastards*
Favourable day for: *alleged axe murderesses*
Scandalous day for: *tennis*

'Lizzie Borden had an axe; gave her mother forty whacks'—only she didn't, for this was the day in 1893 when Lizzie Borden was found innocent of murdering her parents. It is also not a bad day for those of dubious parentage, for on 20 June 1995 religious leaders in Israel announced that the number on a secret list of bastards had dropped from 4,150 to 3,800.

In 1921 on this day, Washington imposed fines on women smoking: $25 plus $100 per cigarette. On 20 June 1949, however, a blow for women's freedom was struck when 'Gorgeous Gussie' Moran caused a scandal at Wimbledon by exposing her lace-trimmed panties under a short tennis skirt.

Other notable events of the day: in 1909, the actor Errol Flynn was born; in 1963, the White House and the Kremlin agreed to set up a hot line; and in 1995, the cultural bureau in Shen-yang, China, banned transvestite shows because they had no artistic merit.

21 June
Feast day of St Aloysius (Luigi Gonzaga), patron saint of youth

Lucky animal: *gorilla*
Lucky fairground ride: *ferris wheel*
Lucky philosophy: *existentialism*

Martha Washington, the first first lady of the USA, was born on this day in 1732, and Benazir Bhutto, the first female leader of Pakistan, was born on the same day in 1953. Other notable birthdays today include Jean-Paul Sartre (1905) and Prince William (1982).

This was the day in 1876 when the first gorilla arrived in Britain, and the day in 1892 when the first ferris wheel was displayed at the World's Columbian Exposition in Chicago.

In 1633, this was a bad day for the earth to go round the sun, because that was when Galileo Galilei was forced by the Inquisition to 'abjure, curse and detest' the Copernician theory. On 21 June 1995 drivers in Shkodër, Albania, refused to pay a new traffic light tax because their city had no traffic lights. Exactly two years later, Mait Lepik won Estonia's first banana-eating contest, consuming 10 bananas in three minutes. To save time, he ate the skins as well.

22 June

Your lucky game: *chess*
Your favourite film genre: *musicals*
Your favourite snack: *a doughnut*

This was a significant day for two of the world's greatest chess-players of the nineteenth century: on 22 June 1837 the great American champion Paul Morphy was born, and on 22 June 1874 his English rival Howard Staunton died. Two others who died today were Judy Garland (in 1969) and Fred Astaire (in 1987). Notable births: Meryl Streep (1951) and George Vancouver (1757), who gave his name to the Canadian city.

It's an important date for lovers of J. R. R. Tolkien's book *The Hobbit*, for on this day in 1342 (in the Shire reckoning) Bilbo Baggins returned to his home at Bag End.

In 1772 on this day, slavery was outlawed in England, but the invention of the day is undoubtedly that of the doughnut in 1847.

Quote of the day: 'Never again'—Wim Alerds, after winning the annual International Pole-sitting Contest in Soltau, near Hamburg, setting a new record of 51 days on top of a pole.

23 June

Official birthday of the Grand Duke of Luxembourg

Lucky animal: *crocodile*
Lucky instrument: *saxophone*
Lucky profession: *hypnotist*

This is the feast day of St Ethelreda (or Audrey), who is celebrated as a virgin although she was married twice. Her second husband, Egfrid, son of King Oswy of Northumbria, tried to change her mind about virginity, and when she refused he released her from the marriage to take holy vows.

Notable events on this day include Adolphe Sax receiving a patent for the saxophone in 1845, President Nixon signing an act in 1972 barring sex discrimination in college sports, the US Supreme Court in 1987 backing the use of hypnosis to obtain testimony; and in 1993, not only did Israel's Supreme Court ban crocodile wrestling, but in England Hom briefs for men went on sale with a horizontal front opening designed to make urinating less stressful.

'Twins' of the day: King Edward VIII and sexologist Alfred Kinsey, both born in 1894.

24 June

Recommended profession: *cosmonaut*
Unlucky disease: *appendicitis*
Lucky king: *Henry VIII*

On 24 June 1947 an airline pilot, Kenneth Arnold, saw—or thought he saw—the first flying saucers: nine disc-shaped objects over Mt Rainier, Washington. This is clearly a good day for novel things in space, because it was also the date in 1983 when Sally Ride became the first American woman in space.

On 24 June 1441, King Henry VI founded Eton College. Henry VIII outdid him by being crowned King of England on this date in 1509, and he celebrated the 31st anniversary of his accession by divorcing his fourth wife, Anne of Cleves, on 24 June 1540. Edward VII was less lucky: on the same date in 1902 his emergency appendectomy operation forced his coronation (scheduled for two days later) to be postponed.

Quote of the day: 'In zero G you can put your trousers on two legs at a time'—Colonel Patrick Baudry of Air France, speaking on 24 June 1985 after his trip on the US space shuttle *Discovery*.

25 June

Good day for: *sheep-shearing*
Bad day for: *a quick game of tennis*
Lucky utensil: *fork*

In 1630 on this day John Winthrop, Governor of Massachusetts, introduced the fork to American dining. Other innovations of the day include barbed wire, patented by Lucien B. Smith of Ohio in 1867, and the car telephone which was first exhibited in Germany in 1925.

It has been a bad day for military men: in 1876 Colonel George Armstrong Custer and 264 men of the 7th US Cavalry were killed by the men of Chief Crazy Horse at the Battle of the Little Bighorn, and in 1797 Nelson lost his arm at the Battle of Santa Cruz.

On 25 June 1969, Pancho Gonzales and Charlie Pasarell played the longest match in the history of the Wimbledon Tennis Championships, lasting 112 games and 5 hours and 12 minutes.

On 25 June 1911, Sir John Throckmorton won a wager of 1,000 guineas that a coat could be made between sunrise and sunset starting with the shearing of a sheep. On 25 June 1996, England beat Germany 3–0 at topless darts.

26 June

Good day for: *moustaches*
Bad day for: *German grammar*
Game of the day: *baseball*

On this day in 1901, professional chauffeurs in Paris struck a blow for personal liberty when they protested at a move to ban them from wearing moustaches.

Achievement of the day: in 1862 Joseph Wells, father of the author H. G. Wells, became the first bowler to take four wickets in four balls in a first-class cricket match.

Invention of the day: in 1797 Charles Newbold patented the first cast-iron plough. It was not an immediate success, being shunned by farmers who feared that iron would poison the soil.

Births of the day: Abner Doubleday (1819), the alleged inventor of American baseball; Zeng Jinlian (1964), who grew a long way up to be the world's tallest woman at 8 feet 1 inch (2.46 metres).

Quote of the day: 'Ich bin ein Berliner'—John F. Kennedy on 26 June 1963. As uttered, the sentence means 'I am a doughnut.' What he meant to say was: 'Ich bin Berliner.'

27 June

Recommended vocation: *king*
Lucky currency: *the yen*
Unlucky accessory: *the tie*

This was the birthday of three European kings: Louis XII (the Just) of France in 1462, Charles IX of France in 1550, and Charles XII of Sweden in 1682.

It s also a good day for money: on 27 June 1871 Japan introduced the yen, and on 27 June 1967 Barclays Bank in Enfield, North London, installed the first cash dispenser in Britain. It was not the only indispensable item of modern life to be introduced on this day, for on 27 June 1929 the first colour television was demonstrated at Bell Laboratories in New York. Another innovation of the day occurred in 1693 with the publication in London of *The Ladies' Mercury*, the first women's magazine.

On 27 June 1988, Dave Hurst and Alan Matthews of Britain became the first blind climbers to scale Mont Blanc, and on 27 June 1997 the aldermen of South Padre Island, Texas, voted to make the wearing of ties illegal.

28 June

Your favourite drink: *champagne*
Your favourite food: *the tomato*
Your favourite animals: *dog, deer and horse*

This was the day in 1682 when Dom Pierre Pérignon invented champagne. More mundanely, it was also the day in 1820 when the tomato was proved to be non-poisonous.

In 1859 on this day the world's first dog show was held in Newcastle-upon-Tyne, attracting 60 entries of pointers and setters. More bestial news of the day: in 1954 a red deer at Milwaukee Zoo died at the age of 26, the oldest known deer. And in 1990 the authorities in Florence decreed that all horses must wear underwear to keep manure off the streets.

It's a fine day in the history of the USA: in 1902, they bought the rights to the Panama Canal from France for $40,000, and in 1950 the American football team beat England 1–0 in the first round of the World Cup. It is also a good day for culture, with the births of Peter Paul Rubens (1577), Jean Jacques Rousseau (1712), Luigi Pirandello (1867) and Mel Brooks (1926).

29 June

Feast day of St Peter, patron saint of fishermen

Good day for: *Nordic women*
Bad day for: *going to the theatre*
Unlucky profession: *policemen*

In 1613 on this day, during a performance of Shakespeare's *Henry VIII*, the Globe Theatre in London burnt down after a cannon, which was set off to mark the king's entrance, set fire to the thatched roof.

On 29 June 1829 Constable William Grantham became the first policeman to be murdered in Britain, when he went to the aid of a woman involved in a fight between drunken Irishmen in London. Another policeman who had a bad day was PC Endacott, who in 1887 wrongfully charged a lady called Miss Cass at Marlborough police station. In court, the magistrate said she had done nothing wrong but warned her not to do it again.

In 1913 on this day, Norway granted women equal rights in parliamentary elections, and on 29 June 1980 Vigdis Finnbogandottir became Iceland's first woman president.

---

30 June

Constitution Day in Mongolia

Good day to: *cross Niagara Falls on a tightrope*
Good way to relax: *spend an extra second in bed*
Unlucky form of punishment: *pillory*

This was the day in 1837 when the pillory was banned as a form of punishment in Britain. Exactly 22 years later, on 30 June 1859, Charles Blondin became the first person to cross Niagara Falls on a tightrope. The rope was 336 metres (1,100 feet) long and the drop, 49 metres (160 feet). In 1972 on this day, the first leap second was added to keep atomic clocks in time with the passage of the earth around the sun.

Two superheroes were born today: the boxer, rapist and ear-biter Mike Tyson in 1966, and Superman himself, who made his first appearance in *Action Comics* on 30 June 1938.

Sports disaster of the day: in 1951, Australia lost 17–0 at soccer to England. Academic event of the day: in 1996, the first World Psychotherapy Congress opened in Vienna.

Quote of the day: 'I Was Raped by the Abominable Snowman' — headline in the US *National Bulletin* on 30 June 1969.

1 July

Lucky vegetable: *spinach*
Unlucky practice: *polygamy*
Good day for: *shoes*

There were two particularly notable births on this day: in 1929, Popeye the (spinach-powered) sailor-man first appeared from the pen of Elzie Sagar; and in 1930 was born Imelda Marcos, who went on to acquire the world's biggest shoe collection as first lady of the Philippines. It was also the birthday, in 1961, of Lady Diana Spencer.

This has generally been a good day for rare events: in 1977, Queen Elizabeth II went to watch the tennis at Wimbledon—something she has not done in the 21 succeeding years—and in 1978 ex-President Nixon made his first public speech since being forced out of office in 1974.

Things made illegal on this day include polygamy, which was outlawed by the US Congress in 1862, and riding a bicycle without a helmet, which was banned in Victoria, Australia, in 1990. To compensate for these restrictions, however, it was also the day in 1931 when the first ice-vending machines were introduced in Los Angeles.

2 July

Recommended profession: *British politician*
Unlucky profession: *American president*
Beware of: *falling alligators*

This was the birthday of two British political party leaders: Sir Alec Douglas-Home (1903), who went on to become prime minister, and Dr David Owen (1938), who didn't, despite becoming the youngest government minister when he was appointed under-secretary to the navy on his 30th birthday. They both had happier memories of the day than US President James Garfield, who was assassinated on 2 July 1881.

It has generally been a good day for shooting people, for in 1994 a Colombian footballer was shot dead by fans after he scored the own goal that led to Colombia's elimination from the World Cup. With all this aggression being vented, it is no surprise that in 1976 the US Supreme Court ruled that the death penalty was not an inherently cruel or unusual punishment.

Weather report: on 2 July 1843, an alligator fell from the sky during a thunderstorm in Charleston, South Carolina.

3 July

Good day for: *being born in Czechoslovakia*
Bad day for: *popular music*
Lucky fruit: *strawberry*

The great Czech composer Leoš Janáček was born on this day in 1854, and the great Czech playwright Franz Kafka followed him in 1883. Tom Stoppard, the Czech-born British playwright, made it a trio on 3 July 1937.

Popular musicians have done far worse, with the deaths of Brian Jones of the Rolling Stones, who drowned at the age of 27 in 1969, and Jim Morrison of the rock band The Doors, who died of heart failure in 1971; and the singer and actor Rudy Vallee died at the age of 84 in 1986.

Two life-changing events happened on this date: in 1806, Michael Keens exhibited the first cultivated strawberry, and in 1928 the first television set in the United States went on sale for $75.

Surreal event of the day: on 3 July 1995, undercover police arrested two clowns who had been peddling drugs in Chapultepec Park in Mexico City. The police arrived at the scene in an ambulance, disguised as paramedics.

4 July

Bad day for: *independence*
Good day to be: *healthy, strong and generous*
Lucky pet: *dog*

Three US ex-presidents died on Independence Day: John Adams and Thomas Jefferson (both in 1826) and James Monroe (in 1831). One president and one king were born today: Calvin Coolidge in 1872 and King Taufa'ahau Tupou IV of Tonga in 1918.

4th of July celebrations include the first public exhibition of electric light in San Francisco in 1876, the first bullfight in the USA in 1884, and Hirofumi Nakajima's victory in the world hot dog eating contest (he ate 24½ in 12 minutes) in New York in 1997.

In 1848 this was the day Marx and Engels chose to publish *The Communist Manifesto*, and in 1984 the UK abolished dog licences. Most ethereally, on 4 July 1973 Pope Paul VI addressed Italian cyclists and praised athletes who 'offer the magnificent show of a healthy, strong, generous youth'.

Quote of the day: 'Nothing of importance happened today'—entry in the diary of King George III for 4 July 1776.

5 July

Tynwald Day in the Isle of Man

···

Bad day for: *speeding*
Lucky profession: *travel agent*
Unlucky animal: *horse*

In 1841, this was the day when Thomas Cook organised his first excursion: a trip from Leicester to Loughborough for members of the temperance movement. In 1865, as if to encourage Mr Cook's rail tours, under the Locomotives and Highways Act England introduced the world's first speed limits for cars—2 mph in towns and 4 mph in the country.

Another great British first came on 5 July 1948 with the birth of Jean Murray at Ashton-in-Makerfield, near Wigan—she was the first baby born on the National Health.

Weather report: in 1643 the United States suffered its earliest recorded tornado, in Essex County, Massachusetts; and in 1891 six horses were killed by hail in Rapid City, South Dakota.

Notable births: Sir Stamford Raffles (1781), who secured the transfer of Singapore to the East India Company in 1819; and Cecil Rhodes (1853), who gave his name to Rhodesia.

---

6 July

···

Unlucky vocation: *King of England*
Lucky drink: *Horlicks*
Lucky disease: *rabies*

Henry II died on this day in 1189, and Edward VI followed him in 1553. On 6 July 1535 Sir Thomas More was executed for treason, and 411 years later Sylvester Stallone was born.

On a healthier note, this was the day in 1885 when Louis Pasteur performed his first inoculation of a human being—against rabies. A year later, Horlick's of Wisconsin offered their malted milk drink to the public for the first time.

Religious events: in 1809 Pope Pius VII was arrested for excommunicating Napoleon; and in 1908 Pope Pius X declared that the UK, USA, Canada and Holland were no longer missionary lands.

Other major events: in 1952, the last tram ran in London; in 1957 John Lennon, 17, met Paul McCartney, 15, for the first time; in 1979 Elizabeth Ryan, the winner of 19 Wimbledon titles, died on the day that Billie Jean King beat her record; and in 1997 a survey showed that 70 per cent of Italians tell 5 to 10 lies every day.

7 July

Lucky drink: *beer*
Lucky band: *the Beatles*
Unlucky item: *women's stockings*

This was the date of birth not only of James McCartney, father of Paul, in 1902, but of Ringo Starr in 1940. They share their birthdays with that rather heavier composer, Gustav Mahler (1860).

Freedom of the day: in 1942, the Vatican allowed women not wearing stockings to enter St Peter's.

Appeal of the day: in 1996, the Sealife Centre in Blackpool put out an urgent appeal for two unwanted Castlemain XXXX stubby bottles as homes for their Australian blue-ringed octopuses. In the wild, they like to nest in such bottles; the neck is just large enough for them to get in while keeping predators out.

Quote of the day: 'We meant to practise but forgot all about it'— Tiina Jussila after she and her husband Jouni had won the first world wife-carrying championship in Sonkajarvi, Finland, in 1996. They won 1000 markka (about £150) plus 44 litres of beer, one for each kilogram she weighed.

8 July

Unlucky profession: *Chinese restaurant waitress*
Lucky item of kit: *boxing gloves*
Lucky name: *Rockefeller*

Both John D. Rockefeller (born 1839), the founder of Standard Oil, and Nelson A. Rockefeller (1908), who became vice-president of the USA, celebrated their birthdays on this day. So did Count Ferdinand von Zeppelin (1838) and Marty Feldman (1933), and so does Nelson Mandela (1918).

Events of the day include: in 1889, the last official bare-knuckle fight for the world heavyweight championship, won by John L. Sullivan by a knock-out in the 75th round; in 1892, the founding of the American Psychological Association; in 1932, the conviction of Harold Davidson, the rector of Stiffkey, Norfolk, for 'disreputable association with women' after he had been accused of making improper suggestions to a waitress in a Chinese restaurant; in 1977, the longest recorded belly-dance— lasting 100 hours—performed by Sabra Starr.

Deaths of the day: AD 810, King Pepin of Italy, son of Charlemagne the Great; 1957, William Cadbury, chocolate king.

9 July

Unlucky profession: *taxi-driver*
Lucky tea-time treat: *doughnut*
Bad day for meeting: *the Pope or extraterrestrials*

The first World Conference of People in Contact with Extraterrestrials began in Miramar, Costa Rica, on this day in 1995; but despite linking hands, chanting and entering a meditative state, the delegates were unable, on the first evening, to persuade any extraterrestrials to come and join them. They did, however, fare better than some people who went to see the Pope in Brazil on 9 July 1980, when seven were killed in a stampede.

Two noteworthy events happened on 9 July 1947: O. J. Simpson was born, and Princess Elizabeth and Lt Philip Mountbatten became engaged to be married.

On this day in 1996, a study of violence in the workplace revealed that the most dangerous job in the USA, in terms of people being murdered at work, is that of taxi-driver.

Invention of the day: the doughnut-cutter, patented by John Blondel of Thomaston, Maine, in 1872.

10 July

Good day for: *apologising*
Bad day for: *fruit-flavoured condoms*
Recommended profession: *tennis-player*

This was the day when two Wimbledon tennis champions were born: Arthur Ashe in 1932 and Virginia Wade in 1945.

The first police radio system went into service on this day in New York in 1933, and the first parking meters in England were installed in 1958. Most innovative of all, Edson P. Clark of Northampton, Massachusetts, patented the indelible pencil in 1866.

Disaster of the day: 24 people were killed by a herd of stampeding elephants in Chandka Forest in India in 1972.

Apology of the day: in 1997 Belgian weather forecasters offered their apologies 'to the inhabitants of the centre of the country who could not enjoy the bright spells we forecast'.

Quote of the date: 'You only put a flavour in when it is something to eat'—Quintin Kintanar, administrator of the Bureau of Food and Drugs in the Philippines, explaining why the authorities threatened to ban fruit-flavoured condoms on 10 July 1995.

11 July

Bad day for: *a headache*
Warm day for: *Eskimos*
Recommended sport: *underwater swimming*

This is the feast day of St Olga (born in 969), the first Russian saint, who was the widow of Prince Igor of Kiev and grandmother of St Vladimir. One of her direct descendants married the daughter of King Harold of England.

In 1938 on this day, Arctic Inuit complained of a heatwave as temperatures hit 19°C. In 1956, the makers of 4711 eau-de-Cologne brought a legal action against one Herr Koelsch of Siegen, West Germany, in an attempt to stop him displaying his phone number prominently on the side of his van; he was a cesspit-emptier and his number was 4711. In 1962, US frogman Fred Baldasare became the first person to swim the English Channel under water.

Quote of the day: 'Boy, have I got a headache. I need an Aspirin before I kill someone'—a woman on American Airlines flight 2074 from Chicago to Newark, New Jersey in 1997. The flight made an emergency landing in Detroit and the woman was escorted from the plane by police. 'The airline took it very seriously,' a spokesman said.

12 July

Art of the day: *photography*
Bad day for: *hamsters*
Disastrous day for: *hippos*

On 12 July 1851, the pioneer photographer Louis Daguerre died, and three years later to the day George Eastman, founder of Kodak, was born.

This is an eventful day for animals: in 1995, the federal postal service in Germany revealed that 2,916 postmen had been bitten by dogs in the previous year at a total medical cost of about £7 million. When, in 1982, a teacher in South Glamorgan fired his starting-pistol at a sports-day rehearsal, the school's pet hamster died of a heart attack. And in 1995, the youngest and oldest hippos in captivity both died on the same day: Tanga, aged 61, died in a zoo in Munich, while at Olmense Zoo in Balen, Belgium, a baby hippo died when its mother rolled over on to it when frightened by a thunderstorm.

Innovations of the day: in 1817 in County Cork, Ireland, the first recorded flower show was held, and in 1859 William Goodale of Massachusetts patented a paper bag manufacturing machine.

13 July

Good day for: *superstition*
Bad day for: *taking a bath*
Lucky shape: *cube*

The composer Arnold Schönberg, who was always superstitious of the number 13, died on Friday 13 July 1951 at 13 minutes to midnight. He was 76 years old (7 + 6 = 13).

This is a good day for inventions: in 1836, the US Patent Office finally awarded patent number 1 (after nearly 10,000 unnumbered patents) to a design for locomotive wheels; in 1898, Marconi patented the wireless.

Birth of the day: Erno Rubik (1944), inventor of the famous cube. Death of the day: Jean-Paul Marat (1793), stabbed by Charlotte Corday in his bath.

Quote of the day: 'I feel pretty stupid'—Bruce Jensen of Bountiful, Utah, on learning in 1995 that his wife of three and a half years, on whom he had just filed a missing-persons report, was a conman called Felix Urioste.

14 July

National day of France and Iraq

Good day for: *breast-feeding*
Lucky food: *boiled egg*
Beware of: *measles*

A number of noteworthy events happened on this day in 1997: in California, Governor Pete Wilson signed a bill guaranteeing women the right to breast-feed in public, and designated August 'Breast-feeding Awareness Month'; in England Malcolm Eccles, who had died five months earlier at the age of 50, had one of his last wishes granted when his ashes were made into an egg-timer; and in Egypt, *Al-Akhbar* newspaper reported the case of a paramedic who collapsed and died when a man who had been pronounced dead opened the lid of his coffin and started shouting for help.

Invention of the day: the tape-measure in a circular case was patented in 1868 by A. J. Fellows.

Other notable events: on this day in 1823 King Kamehameha of Hawaii and his queen both died of measles while visiting Britain, and in 1945 the ban was lifted on Allied troops fraternising with German women.

15 July

Dish of the day: *salami sandwiches with margarine*
Drink of the day: *non-alcoholic*
Lucky animal: *duck-billed platypus*

This is a day with many gastronomic connotations. In 1869 margarine was patented in Paris, for use by the French navy, by Hippolyte Mège-Mouriès. (He may have been inspired by the Marseillaise, which was adopted as the French national anthem on the same day in 1795.) In 1948, the British branch of Alcoholics Anonymous was formed, and in 1996 Ettore Szokoll, 30, was suspended as invigilator at a high school in Bergamo, Italy, for having sandwiches delivered to students containing the answers neatly hidden between slices of salami.

It has been a day of extremes: it was the date of birth in 1701 of Pierre Joubert, who went on to become the oldest-known Canadian at 113 years and 124 days, and the date of the death in 1940 of Robert Wadlow, the world's tallest man at 8 feet 11.1 inches.

In 1922, this was the day that New York Zoo gave the American public their first sight of a duck-billed platypus.

16 July

Lucky profession: *traffic warden*
Lucky number: *72*
Bad day for: *lovers*

On this day in 1439, kissing was banned in England. Other unpleasant things to happen on 16 July were the installation of the world's first parking meter, in Oklahoma City in 1935, and the detonation of the first atom bomb in New Mexico in 1945.

The world had been given a little more stability in 1867, when Joseph Monier, a Parisian gardener, received a patent for reinforced concrete; and a blow was struck for religious tolerance in 1924 with the birth of Bess Myerson, who went on to become the first Jewish Miss America in 1945.

Achievement of the day: in 1981, Shukuni Sasaki established a new world record by setting 72 plates spinning at the same time.

Economic event of the day: in 1661 Sweden became the first European country to issue banknotes.

Birthdays of the day: painter Sir Joshua Reynolds (1723), dancer Ginger Rogers (1911), popcorn pioneer Orville Redenbacher (1907).

17 July

Good day for: *sewing*
Bad day for: *Santa Claus*
Confusing day for: *moles*

On this day in 1408, a sow was hanged in the French town of Pont-de-l'Arche 'for the crime of having murdered and killed a little child'. Another animal to have died on this date was Modoc the elephant, who passed away in 1975 in Santa Clara, California, at the age of 78, the oldest-verified non-human mammal. Interestingly, it was on 17 July 1997 that the scientific journal *Nature* published a paper showing that the African golden mole is more closely related to the elephant than to the garden mole.

On 17 July 1995, there was a major dispute at the 32nd World Santa Claus Conference in Copenhagen when Finnish Santas boycotted the event because the 132 other delegates would not recognise their claim that Finland is the only true home of Santa.

Invention of the day: the sewing-machine, patented in 1790 by Thomas Saint of London. Illumination of the day: Arco, Idaho, became the first city lit by nuclear power in 1955.

18 July

199th day of the year (200th in a leap year)

Good day for: *cricketers*
Bad day for: *painters*
Mixed day for: *novelists*

W. G. Grace (1848) and Dennis Lillee (1949) were both born on this day; Michelangelo Merisi da Caravaggio (1610) and Jean-Antoine Watteau (1721) both died; William Makepeace Thackeray was born (1811) and Jane Austen died (1817). On 18 July 1966, the cosmologist Carl Sagan celebrated his billionth second on earth.

It has been a curious day for popes: in 1536 the Pope was declared to have no authority in England, but in 1870, 18 July was the day popes officially became infallible when the First Vatican Council proclaimed the dogma of papal infallibility.

Bad decision of the day: in 1969 Mary Jo Kopechne accepted a lift home from a party at Martha's Vineyard in Senator Edward Kennedy's Oldsmobile. Omission of the day: in 1988 Margaret Thatcher was the only Western leader not to send Nelson Mandela a 70th birthday card.

19 July

Unlucky name: *Mary*
Bad day for: *spelling*
Beware of: *rabid men*

At the first women's rights assembly in Seneca Falls, New York, on 19 July 1851 Miss Amelia Bloomer introduced the undergarments that were to be known by her name. They arrived in time to have been worn by Lizzie Borden, the alleged axe murderess, who was born on this day in 1860. Another famous name with this birthday (in 1814) was Samuel Colt, inventor of the Colt revolver.

Sinkings of the day: in 1545 the flagship of Henry VIII, the *Mary Rose*, sank in the Solent, and in 1969 Mary Jo Kopechne drowned at Chappaquiddick in Edward Kennedy's car.

Still in America, this was the day in 1911 when the US Board of Geographic Names finally gave up its 20-year battle to persuade Pittsburgh to drop its final *h*; and in 1918 baseball was declared a 'nonessential occupation' under the 'work or fight' law.

In 1995 in Suzhou, China, a rabid man bit four people in random attacks—he had been bitten by two rabid dogs a month earlier.

20 July

Feast day of St Margaret of Antioch, patron saint of pregnant women

Good day for: *professional sport*
Bad day for: *armed robbery*
Recommended excursion: *outer space*

In 1858, the baseball match between New York and Brooklyn was the first at which spectators were charged a fee, and in 1885 the British parliament legalised professional football.

This is also an important date in space travel: in 1960, two Russian dogs became the first creatures to survive a trip into space; in 1969, the first men landed on the moon; and in 1976, the US Viking 1 made the first unmanned landing on Mars.

On this day in 1995, an armed robber handed a note demanding money to a shopkeeper in Groningen, the Netherlands. The man scribbled his reply—'Sod off'—and the robber fled.

Futile gesture of the day: in 1910, the Christian Endeavour Society of Missouri started a campaign to ban all kissing in films between non-relatives.

On 20 July 1970 the first baby was born on Alcatraz island.

21 July

Good day to: *be shot at*
Bad day for: *keeping fit*
Unlucky number: *57*

This was the day in 1798 when Napoleon defeated the Mamelukes at the Battle of the Pyramids in Egypt. Sadly, they were much too early to benefit from the skills of a man who died on this day in 1957: Bernard Spooner, inventor of the bullet-proof jacket.

Another who died on this date was James Fixx, who did more than anyone else to popularise jogging. He dropped dead of a heart attack at the age of 52—while out jogging. Still on the subject of deaths, it's worth noting that there were a record 57 murders in New York on 21 July 1972.

The sport of the day is camel-racing. In 1997, the town of Boulia, Queensland, was the first in Australia to host a camel-race on which bets could be placed.

It's a bad day for air travel: in 1919, a dirigible crashed through a bank skylight in Chicago killing 13, and in 1988 a bull attacked a landing Boeing 737 at Baruda airport, India.

22 July

Dish of the day: *roast lamb*
Lucky profession: *rat-catcher*
Auspicious mode of transport: *helicopter*

In 1284, according to legend, 22 July marked the arrival in the rat-infested village of Hamelin of the Pied Piper.

Births of the day include those of Philip the Handsome of Spain (husband of Juana the Mad) in 1478, and of the Reverend William Spooner, unwitting inventor of the spoonerism, in 1844.

Good advice of the day: in 1996 the *Workplace Health and Safety Guide* was published in Queensland, Australia, which included a warning not to 'place any part of one's body in the mouth of a crocodile'.

Natural disaster of the day: in 1918 in the Wasatch National Park in Utah, 504 sheep were killed by lightning.

Achievement of the day: in 1983, Dick Smith completed the first solo flight round the world in a helicopter.

Sporting event of the day: in 1894 the first motor-car race was run from Paris to Rouen.

23 July
Neptunalia in ancient Rome

....

Lucky part of the body: *G-spot*
Lucky sport: *roller-blading*
Lucky concept: *cyberspace*

This was the day in 1997 when 'G-spot', 'roller-blading' and 'cyberspace' all became officially part of the English language with their inclusion in the supplement to the *Oxford English Dictionary*.

Births of the day: Haile Selassie, Emperor of Ethiopia (1891), and Schottzie Schott, dog mascot of the Cincinnati Reds (1982).

Inventions of the day: in 1829 William Austin Burt patented the 'typographer', the first typewriter, and in 1904 Charles E. Menches invented the ice-cream cone.

In 1931 on this day, France announced that she couldn't afford to send a team to the 1932 Olympics, and in 1946 Britain introduced bread rationing because of a poor harvest.

Quote of the day: 'Rational man, *Homo sapiens*. Subspecies: scientific workers'—sign in Moscow Zoo on a cage occupied in 1995 by three scientists protesting against their poor pay.

─────────────────────────────────────

24 July

....

Good day for: *windows*
Bad day for: *moustaches*
Beware of: *whirlpools*

This was a mixed day for opinion polls. The good news is that it was the date of the first opinion poll, carried out in Delaware before the presidential election contest between Andrew Jackson and John Quincy Adams in 1824. The bad news is that it made the wrong prediction.

In 1851 on this day, the window tax was finally abolished in Britain after being in force for over 150 years. Two years later Captain Matthew Webb, who had been the first man to swim the English Channel, drowned while attempting the whirlpool rapids of Niagara Falls.

In 1995 workers at Hintex, a textile company in Indonesia, went on strike after a new rule banned male employees from wearing moustaches.

Exaggeration of the day: 'The greatest week in the history of the world since the Creation'—Richard Nixon's comment on the return of the Apollo XI moon-landing astronauts in 1969.

─────────────────────────────────────

25 July

Good day to: *cross the Channel*
Lucky profession: *typist*
Beware of: *toothache*

On this day in 1909, Louis Blériot made the first crossing of the English Channel by plane, and exactly fifty years later the same date was chosen for the first Channel crossing by hovercraft.

Other firsts on this date include the first inter-college billiards match in America (between Harvard and Yale) in 1860; the first bikini worn at a fashion show, in Paris in 1946; the first test-tube baby to be born (Louise Brown at Oldham General Hospital) in 1978; the first woman to walk in space (Svetlana Savitskaya) in 1984.

Death of the day: British army surgeon Major-General James Barry in 1843, who was subsequently discovered to have been a woman.

Achievement of the day: in 1995 Yu Qian, a Chinese dentist, unveiled his 2.5 metre high tower made of 28,000 diseased human teeth—his aim was to raise awareness of dental hygiene.

Contest of the day: in 1888 Frank McGurrin launched touch-typing by defeating an official stenographer in a typing contest.

26 July

Lucky profession: *film director*
Good day for: *numbers*
Bad day for: *eternity*

This was the day in 1995 when the eternal flame went out in the Russian town of Taganrog. It had been burning to honour the memory of those killed in the Second World War, and went out because the town had not paid its gas bill.

26 July 1956 saw the unveiling of ERNIE, the electronic random number indicator equipment that was to pick the winning numbers of Britain's Premium Bonds, and in 1965 the British Post Office switched to numbers-only phone dialling.

Two film directors were born on 26 July: Blake Edwards (1922) and Stanley Kubrick (1928). One young woman died on this day: the first lady of Argentina, Eva Perón, in 1952 at the age of 33.

The first recorded women's cricket match was played on 26 July 1745 when, according to a contemporary account, 'eleven maids from Hambledon beat eleven maids from Bramley' at Gosden Common in Surrey.

27 July

Feast day of St Pantaleon, patron saint of medicine

Unlucky number of the day: *7*
Flavour of the day: *mint*
Disease of the day: *lung cancer*

St Pantaleon is thought to have been court physician to the emperor Galerius. He was rescued from a life of self-indulgence by a Christian friend, persecuted by Diocletian and put to death around 304 by beheading when six other methods of execution had failed.

In 1837 on this day, the US Mint opened at Charlotte, North Carolina, and seven years later to the day it was destroyed by fire.

Winston Churchill made his final appearance in the House of Commons on this day in 1964, and exactly 16 years later the deposed Shah of Iran died in Cairo. In 1586, Sir Walter Raleigh brought the first tobacco from Virginia to England; in 1988 the city of Boston, Massachusetts, had its worst traffic jam for 30 years; and in 1990 Zsa Zsa Gabor began a three-day gaol sentence for slapping a police officer.

Sporting event of the day: the first recorded women's national athletics championships were held in Vienna on 27 July 1918.

28 July

Good day for: *dancing a foxtrot to the music of J. S. Bach*
Bad day for: *drug-dealers*
Seasonal vegetable: *potato*

This was generally a terrible day for music, with the deaths of J. S. Bach in 1750 and Antonio Vivaldi in 1741. In 1914, however, Harry Fox made up for it by inventing the foxtrot. Another eponym associated with this day is Earl S. Tupper, the inventor of Tupperware, who was born on 28 July 1907.

It's the ideal day for hamburger and chips: the hamburger was created by Louis Lassing in Connecticut on 28 July 1900 and the potato was introduced to Europe by Sir Thomas Harriot on 28 July 1586. The other innovation of the day was the singing telegram, the first of which was delivered in New York on this day in 1933.

In 1890 Scotland beat England in the first water polo international, and in 1916 Britain banned the import of cocaine and opium. In 1962, Simon Paterson became the first Englishman to swim the Channel under water.

29 July

Feast day of St Martha, patron saint of housewives

Good day for: *women's fashions*
Bad day for: *Spanish ships*
Inauspicious day for: *getting married*

'And Jesus answered and said unto her, Martha, Martha, thou art careful and troubled about many things' (Luke x. 41)—which may be why she is regarded as the patroness not only of housewives but also of those actively engaged in the care of the needy. St Martha was the sister of Lazarus.

This was the day in 1588 that the Spanish Armada was defeated by the English under Sir Francis Drake. It was also the day in 1715 when a hurricane sank ten Spanish treasure galleons off the coast of Florida. Another doomed venture that began today was the marriage in 1981 of Prince Charles and Lady Diana Spencer.

On 29 July 1926, the London County Council praised modern women's fashions on grounds of hygiene.

Births of the day: Rasputin (1872), Mussolini (1883).

Deaths: Olaf II of Norway (1030), Umberto I of Italy (1900).

30 July

Good day for: *cycling*
Bad day for: *obesity*
Lucky surname: *Moore*

This was the birthday of both the sculptor Henry Moore (1898) and the piano accompanist Gerald Moore (1899). Other births include Emily Brontë (1818) and Arnold Schwarzenegger (1947).

It was the day in 1966 when England won the World Cup—not an original feat, since Uruguay had won the first World Cup in 1930 on the same date.

Two notable publishing ventures began on this day: the first paperbacks were brought out by Penguin in 1935, and the first issue of the *Beano* appeared in 1938.

In 1968 Don Jones, the public defender of California state, was fined for being too fat—he weighed 238 lb. On this day in 1971, Ronald J. Dossenbach set off on his world-record cycle ride across Canada from Vancouver to Halifax. It took him 13 days, 15 hours and 4 minutes.

Bravery of the day: in 1918 one Captain Sarret of France made the first parachute jump from an aeroplane.

31 July

Good day for: *vehicular innovation*
Remarkable day for: *sexual excess*
Sensitive day for: *dead women*

In 1809 on this day, the first working railroad track was laid in the United States. Made of wood and designed for horse-drawn wagons, it was manufactured in Philadelphia. In 1922 Ralph Samuelson, aged 22, became the first person to ride on water skis; and in 1971 the first lunar roving vehicle, which quickly became known as the 'moon buggy', was driven on the moon by David Scott and Jim Irwin.

On 31 July 1995, the *Al-Watan* newspaper in Kuwait reported the case of a man who had been rushed to hospital with back pain and exhaustion after making love to his 17-year-old wife six times a day in the week after their wedding. 'He was pale and energyless and could not speak,' a neighbour said.

Quote of the day: 'Single ladies of the older generation have also said they don't want to be messed around with by a man they don't know' — Barbara Butler, on opening Martha's Funerals, Britain's first all-female funeral parlour, on 31 July 1996.

1 August

Parents' Day in Zaïre

Recommended vocation: *Roman emperor*
Lucky element: *oxygen*
Good day for: *introductions*

Two Roman emperors were born on this day: Claudius in 10 BC and Publius Helvius Pertinax, the son of a freed slave, in AD 126.

On 1 August 1793 the kilogram was the first metric unit to be introduced in France; in 1944 post codes were introduced in Germany; and in 1960 the 'twist' was introduced by Chubby Checker. Sir Joseph Priestley announced his discovery of oxygen on this day in 1774.

Among things that have ended today are the British halfpenny, imperial currency, which ceased to be legal tender in 1969; slavery, which was abolished in the British Empire in 1833; and Liz Taylor's marriage to Richard Burton, whom she divorced for the second time in 1976.

On 1 August 1995 the High Court in Hong Kong ruled that Michelangelo's *David* is not obscene, and on the same day an Egyptian newspaper reported the deaths of six people who had jumped into a well in the village of Nazlet Emaha to save a chicken.

2 August

National Tree-planting Day in Lesotho

....

Good day for: *jumping*
Unlucky poker hand: *two pairs—aces and eights*
Unlucky vocation: *king*

On this day in 1100, William Rufus was shot by an arrow while out hunting—suspicion centred on his younger brother, who became Henry I. On 2 August 1589, Henry III of France was stabbed to death by a mad monk. Another person killed today was Wild Bill Hickok, shot from behind by Jack McCall in 1876 while playing poker. His fatal hand was a pair of aces and a pair of eights.

Bob Beamon, the first long-jumper to clear 29 feet, was born on this day in 1946, and the first parachute jump in the USA was accomplished on 2 August 1819. In 1875, Britain's first roller-skating rink opened in Belgravia, London. And another sporting first happened in Spain in 1987 when Luis Reina became the first matador to appear in a bull-ring with an advertiser's logo on his suit.

Invasion of the day: Iraq occupied Kuwait in 1990.

3 August

....

Good day for: *traffic control*
Bad day for: *caterpillars*
Lucky direction: *vertical*

The first aerial crop-spraying happened on this day in 1921, when a plane from the Ohio Agricultural Research Station sprayed a catalpa grove infested with leaf caterpillars. That was not the only aerial innovation of the day, for in 1954 the first vertical take-off and landing prototype was flown.

Back on the ground, in 1925 a court in Indiana ordered a motorist who had killed a pedestrian to spend an hour alone with the body; and in 1926 the first electric traffic lights in England were set up in Piccadilly Circus.

Birth of the day: Elisha Graves Otis (1811), lift pioneer.

Death of the day: Sir Richard Arkwright (1792), inventor of the water-powered spinning-mill.

Quote of the day: 'The lamps are going out all over Europe; we shall not see them lit again in our lifetime'—Sir Edward Grey, on 3 August 1914.

4 August

Unlucky profession: *fireman*
Unlucky religion: *Christianity*
Beware of: *Leninism*

This was the day in 1966 when John Lennon said that the Beatles were more popular than Jesus Christ; Beatles records were promptly banned in some American states and in South Africa. A 15-year-old Russian boy paid more severely for another disrespectful act in 1996 when he attempted to climb a statue of Lenin in Khorinsk, Siberia. The statue was not fixed on its pedestal and it toppled over, killing him.

On 4 August 1995 an American woman, Joy Glassman, was reported to have been arrested and released on $10,000 bail after admitting to having started five fires in an attempt to help her son's career as a fire-fighter.

Births of the day: Percy Bysshe Shelley (1792) and Queen Elizabeth, the Queen Mother (1900).

Death of the day: Hans Christian Andersen (1875).

Invention of the day: champagne, by Dom Pérignon in 1693.

5 August

Beginning of the British oyster season

Good day to: *celebrate the New Year*
Pastime of the day: *underwater burial*
Lucky extra: *hairy chest*

Villagers in Berchules, Spain, celebrated the New Year on 5 August 1995—plans for festivities on the actual New Year's Eve had been postponed when the town was blacked out by a 13-hour power cut. When the event was rerun, they used white mousse as snow.

According to a survey in Brazil published on 5 August 1996, 73 per cent of men and 38 per cent of women still have an active sex life after the age of 60. Hairy chests were considered attractive by 82.5 per cent of women. Meanwhile, on the very same day in Shanghai a lovesick man climbed into a tiger's cage at the zoo and begged the animal to eat him. The tiger took a bite from his neck before it was sedated and the man rescued.

This was the day in 1926 when Harry Houdini stayed in a coffin under water for one and a half hours, and in 1970 when penalty kicks were first used as a tie-breaker in an English football match.

6 August

Good day for: *advertising*
Bad day for: *pot-bellies*
Lucky number: *2,367,234*

Shakespeare's wife and one of his friends died on this day: Anne Hathaway in 1623 and Ben Jonson in 1637. One US president's wife was born — Edith Kermit Carow Roosevelt (Theodore Roosevelt's second wife), in 1861; and one died — Ellen Wilson (Woodrow's spouse), in 1914.

On this day in 1995 a group of Malaysians completed a 55.6-kilometre line of 2,367,234 coins, ending in front of the Sultan Abdul Samad building in Kuala Lumpur to set a new world record.

Invention of the day: the spray-on latex condom, demonstrated in 1996 by Karl Machhamer of Austria.

Quotes of the day: (1) 'Worth a guinea a box', the world's first advertising slogan, which appeared on 6 August 1859 to promote Beecham's powders; (2) 'Photographs in the press of pot-bellied policemen have given the police a bad name', Indian police chief V. N. Deshmukh explaining why 110 fat officers had been forced to attend a day-long 'pot-bellies seminar' on 6 August 1996.

7 August

Good day for: *going round in circles*
Excellent day for: *extraterrestrials*
Vegetable of the day: *potato*

In 1556 on this day, the first unidentified flying object was seen over Basle in Switzerland. Exactly 440 years later, William Hill in London slashed the odds against NASA confirming the existence of intelligent life in space within the next 12 months from 500 to 1 down to 25 to 1.

In 1840 this was a good day for children, as the British parliament passed a bill forbidding the indenturing of child chimney-sweeps. Exactly 18 years later, the rules of Australian football were formulated.

Two other important nineteenth-century events on this date: in 1820 the first potatoes were planted in Hawaii, and in 1888 Theophilus van Kannel patented the revolving door.

Births of the day: Mata Hari, dancer, courtesan and spy, in 1876; Garrison Keillor, American author, in 1942. Death of the day: Schottzie Schott, dog mascot of the Cincinnati Reds, at the age of nine in 1991.

8 August

Good day to: *contemplate resignation*
Lucky language: *Portuguese*
Investment tip of the day: *topless bars*

On 8 August 1973, Vice-President Spiro Agnew said that accusations against him of financial irregularities were 'damned lies' and he would not resign. He resigned shortly after. On 8 August 1974, President Nixon announced his own resignation.

On 8 August 1995, Rick's Cabaret of Houston, Texas, became the first topless bar to be traded on the stock market.

On 8 August 1996, the Society for the Portuguese Language set up a commission to halt the influx of English words. 'Franchising', 'mall' and 'shopping centre' were deemed particularly offensive.

Quote of the day: 'This makes no sense, has no redeeming social value and offers no prize money'—Mark Soifer, public relations officer for Ocean City, New Jersey, when asked to explain the success and longevity of the annual 'Miss Crustacean pageant'. The 1996 event had just been won by Copa Crabana, a hermit crab dressed in gold and blue feathers.

9 August

Nagasaki Memorial Day in Japan

Good day for: *breasts*
Bad day to: *collect elephant dung*
Lucky number: 6.023×10^{23}

This was the birthday in 1776 of Amedeo Avogadro, whose law states that equal volumes of different gases at the same temperature and pressure contain the same number of molecules. This number, which is 6.023×10^{23} per mole, is known as 'Avogadro's number'.

Britain's first nudist beach opened in Brighton on 9 August 1979, and on 9 August 1995 research in Britain showed that women who are built symmetrically face a lower risk of breast cancer than asymmetric ones. Exactly one year later Vicky Yun, an image consultant in Singapore, said that by 2025 Singaporean women's average bust sizes would have increased from 81 to 91 centimetres.

Death of the day: in 1996 a 60-year-old Nigerian was trampled to death in the village of Bokkos as he tried to collect fresh dung from beneath an elephant for use in traditional medicines.

10 August

Lucky name: *Magellan*
Lucky substance: *cement*
Unlucky profession: *spy*

On hearing that Kim Philby was a spy, a traitor and a homosexual, the queen cancelled his OBE on this day in 1965. Another disgraced character lost an honour on this day in 1981, when the Richard Nixon Museum in San Clement closed.

This was the day in 1519 that Magellan's five ships set sail in their attempt to circumnavigate the globe; and on the same day in 1990 the Magellan spacecraft landed on Venus.

Punishment of the day: on 10 August 1995 village elders in Dukusari, Indonesia, ordered a 57-year-old man to haul 100 sacks of cement as punishment for committing incest with his 25-year-old daughter. The cement would be used to build the village hall, long-delayed because of a cement shortage.

Invention of the day: in 1889 the screw-top bottle was patented by Dan Rylands of Barnsley, Yorkshire.

Mozart finished *Eine kleine Nachtmusik* on 10 August 1787.

11 August

Feast day of St Clare, patron saint of television

Your lucky planet: *Mars*
Your lucky pet: *not a parrot*
Bad day to: *attempt suicide*

St Clare of Assisi (died 1253) experienced, during an illness, a vision of the nativity in Bethlehem in the form of a moving picture on her bedroom wall. She was therefore made patron saint of television.

On 11 August 1995, Henry the parrot was barred from the Avenue and Victoria bowls club in Leamington Spa. Its habit of shrieking, 'You're a yard short, a yard short' was irritating contestants in the preliminary rounds of the English Women's Bowls Championship.

On the very same day, in a gaol in Oklahoma, Robert Brecheen was rushed to the prison hospital to have his stomach pumped after he had taken a drug overdose. He was then taken back to prison and executed by lethal injection.

This was the day in 1877 when astronomer Asaph Hall discovered Deimos, one of the two moons of Mars. It was also the day in 1711 of the first race meeting at Ascot.

12 August

Bad day for: *chess*
Worse day for: *football*
Day of mixed fortunes for: *rare animals*

On 12 August 1851 Isaac Singer received a patent for his sewing-machine, and in 1877 Thomas Edison made the first recording on his 'Edisonphone', the first gramophone, when he recorded 'Mary had a little lamb'.

Mary's lamb was not the only animal in the news on this day. In 1883, the last quagga in the world died in a zoo in Amsterdam; in 1949, starlings perching on the minute hand of Big Ben caused it to lose nearly five minutes; and 12 August 1980 saw the first panda cub to be born in captivity, in Mexico.

Wilhelm Steinitz, the first official world chess champion, died on this day in 1900, having been certified insane the previous year. And on 12 August 1995, a paper delivered to the American Psychological Association produced evidence showing that soccer players who repeatedly use their heads to hit the ball risk suffering impaired mental skills.

13 August

Good day for: *chewing gum*
Bad day for: *being hanged*
Repulsive day for: *snails*

This is a good day for books, films and television: it was the birthday of William Caxton (1422), John Logie Baird (1888) and Alfred Hitchcock (1899). It was also the date of the death in 1991 of Jack Ryan, inventor of the Barbie Doll.

On 13 August 1997, Hong Kong businessman Leung Ka-ching successfully appealed against a fine that had been imposed on him for chewing gum in court. He claimed that he had been doing it so as to show respect for the court by having fresh breath. On the very same day, the official Laotian news agency reported that farmers were successfully using pig manure as snail repellent on their rice crops.

Innovation of the day: the first taxi-cab in New York in 1907.

Deaths of the day: Peter Allen and John Welby, the last people to be hanged in Britain, in 1964.

Quote of the day: 'It was the very thing I desired'—Enrico Caruso, in 1908, when his wife ran off with another man.

14 August

Liberty Tree Day in Massachusetts

Bad day for: *Barry Manilow*
Unlucky form of transport: *hot-air balloon*
Confusing day for: *cows*

In 1908 on this day the first international beauty contest was staged in Folkestone, with six English, three French, one Irish, one American and one Austrian girl 'and a number of fishergirls from Boulogne'; in 1932 dog film star Rin Tin Tin died; and in 1961, the East Germans started building the Berlin Wall.

The worst hot-air balloon disaster in history left 13 dead when two balloons collided near Alice Springs, Australia, in 1989; and in 1997 a genetic study published in *Nature* showed that cows are more closely related to whales than to pigs.

Quote of the day: 'One viewer who complained about a man wearing an artificial penis on his nose in the *Big Breakfast* was informed that this was not the case and the man was in fact doing an impression of Barry Manilow'—Independent Television Commission report on viewers' complaints, 14 August 1995.

15 August

Mothers' Day in Costa Rica

Good day for: *baldness*
Bad day for: *robbing a petrol station*
Unlucky Scottish king: *Macbeth*

Don Bradman played his last innings on this day in 1948 and was out for a duck. Jeffrey Alan McLeod, 29, was even more unlucky in 1996 in his bid to rob a petrol station in Florida: his escape car ran out of petrol 20 miles down the road. A spokesman for the local sheriff's office said, after arresting him: 'When you set out to rob a gas station, you're supposed to fill up the tank before you rob the clerk.'

15 August 1996 was also the day when SCUB, the Slovak Club of the Unjustly Bald, announced new potions for promoting premature hair loss and to encourage a shiny look: 'Yellow cream for a fuzzy knee-cap look, orange for Franciscan monk, blue for Kojak.'

This was the day in 1057 when Macbeth, King of Scotland, was killed by Malcolm, son of King Duncan, and the day in 1927 when the length of motor vehicles in England was limited to 27 feet and 6 inches.

16 August

Good day for: *Madonna*
Bad day for: *Elvis*
Worrying day for: *windshield-washers*

American legends have fared badly today with the death of Babe Ruth at the age of 53 in 1948, and of Elvis Presley, aged 42, in 1977. It has not been a good day for Elvis fans, either: on 16 August 1996 Lynn Siddick and her son-in-law Ian Goldhill laid a bet of £20 at odds of 1,000–1 that Elvis Presley would appear in person at a concert in Memphis later that day. They lost.

Madonna (Ciccone) was born on 16 August 1958 and married actor Sean Penn on her 27th birthday in 1985. Exactly three years later, Mayor Ed Koch of New York announced that he planned to wipe out street-corner car windshield-washers.

Quote of the day: 'My old men are bald-headed with just a fringe around the back. You can't charge them much, can you?'—Valerie Prate, a New Zealand hairdresser, on being told in 1996 that her 'pensioner special' haircut offer of $5 for men and $15 for women was illegal discrimination by gender.

17 August

Sport of the day: *camel-racing*
Dangerous sport of the day: *sunbathing*
Bad day for: *margins*

This day in 1601 saw the birth of the French mathematician Pierre de Fermat, whose notorious 'last theorem' was finally proved in 1997. Fermat claimed he had the proof himself, but that the margin of his maths book was too small for him to write it down.

Deaths of the day: (1) in 1896 Miss Bridget Driscoll of Croydon, Surrey, became the first pedestrian to be killed by a motor vehicle in Britain, despite a 4 mph speed limit; (2) in 1995 Danish tourist Migerzen Molganson, 19, was killed in Bangkok while sunbathing at a swimming pool, by a man falling on her from the 18th floor of a neighbouring block of flats. It is not known whether he jumped or fell by accident.

Sporting news: in 1995, the Brazilian football league banned players from running behind the goal and pretending to make phone calls after scoring a goal; in 1997 the first camel-races in northern Europe were held in Berlin.

18 August

Cultural highlights: *music and clean toilets*
Good behaviour award: *bull in china shop*
Lucky animal: *sheep*

On 18 August 1996, the Clean Toilets Education Campaign was launched in Singapore. Clean public toilets and appreciation of music were identified as markers of a more gracious society. On the same day, Philippe Cailleau of Fréchou, France, won the Melon-seed Spitters' World Championship with a spit of almost 7 metres. It was a long way short of the world record, but he had been spitting into the wind.

Meanwhile, at the National Museum of Women in the Arts in Washington, 18 August 1996 marked the start of an exhibit called 'Love Conquers War' by Lindee Climo. It featured 23 paintings, all modelled on famous classical works, but with the human figures in them replaced by sheep.

An old cliché was disproved on this day in 1997 when Raja, a three-year-old bull elephant, backed into a china shop in Woburn, Bedfordshire, but negotiated his way round the premises and out again without breaking anything.

19 August

Significant day for: *taxis*
Bad day for: *fish*
Fortunate day for: *a birthday*

In 1996, the Thai parliament debated whether this was the birthday of the prime minister. Old official documents said Banharn Silpa-archa was born on 20 July 1932, but opposition members accused him of changing it to 19 August on the advice of a fortune-teller.

Electric-powered taxis were introduced in London on this day in 1897, but withdrawn three years later. On 19 August 1997, a Belgian thief phoned for a taxi to help him get his loot—two garbage bags full of silverware—home. He gave the driver his real name and was taken to his home address, where the police arrested him soon after.

19 August 1941 was the date of US patent no. 2253125, for a firing mechanism in a fishing hook invented by H. Heineke and others. When the bait is taken, the gun fires, killing or stunning the fish.

Quote of the day: 'We simply cannot have roasted swans'—Derek Deane, telling dancers in the English Royal Ballet production of *Swan Lake* in 1997 to go away and lose their suntans.

20 August

Good day to: *owe much to few*
Catch of the day: *bream*
Beware of: *ice-picks, toilet-paper and football fans*

Assassination of the day: Ramón del Rio (alias Jacques Mornard), a Spanish Communist, fatally wounded Leon Trotsky with an ice-pick on 20 August 1940.

Fatal accident of the day: Turkish football fan Mustafa Portakal accidentally killed his son Ilker when he fired a shotgun in celebration of his country's 6–4 win over Wales in a World Cup qualifier in 1997.

Will of the day: also on 20 August 1997, it was reported that champion angler Peter Hodge from Somerset had made a will specifying that his ashes be mixed with groundbait and fed to the bream at his favourite fishing spot.

Quotes of the day: (1) 'Never in the field of human conflict was so much owed by so many to so few'—Winston Churchill, 20 August 1940; (2) 'We cannot leave the toilets open to view because of human rights considerations; nor can we leave the toilets without paper'—a police spokesman in Japan on 20 August 1996, after a suspect committed suicide by stuffing toilet-paper down his throat.

21 August

Good day for: *one-legged flamingoes*
Bad day for: *eye contact*
Litigious day for: *non-smokers*

The major events of this day are as follows:

1923: the city of Kalamazoo, Michigan, forbade dancers to stare into their partners' eyes.

1928: Joseph Schenck, the head of United Artists, said that talkies were just a fad and would not last.

1968: Warsaw Pact troops invaded Czechoslovakia.

1976: Mary Langdon became Britain's first female fireman.

1997: a plastic artificial leg was fitted to a pink flamingo in Lincoln Park Zoo, Illinois. The flamingo, known only as B9720, was believed to be the world's first with an artificial leg.

1997: retired colonel Richard J. Thomas filed a suit asking a judge to declare the smoke from his wife's cigarettes to be a cancer-causing pollutant under the federal Clean Air Act. He said he'd drop the action if she gave up smoking.

Royal births: King William IV (1765), Princess Margaret (1930).

22 August

Good day for: *monsters*
Bad day for: *fussy eaters*
Four-letter word of the day: *'step'*

On this day in the year 565, St Columba reported seeing a monster in Loch Ness, the earliest alleged sighting. In 1902 Teddy Roosevelt became the first US president to ride in a car, and in 1911 the *Mona Lisa* was stolen from the Louvre and more people queued to see the empty space than had ever come to see the painting.

Births of the day include Honor Blackman (1926), who was to become the first female lead in the television series *The Avengers,* and Norman Schwarzkopf (1934), who was to be the male lead in the Gulf War of 1991.

On 22 August 1996, the Italian government ordered birth registry offices to stop using the word 'step-child' because it carried negative connotations. On 22 August 1997 Hiromichi Katsuki, 50, was charged with stealing a boxed lunch from a car. He admitted taking a total of 80 lunches at a rate of about two a day—all homemade 'because I am fussy about flavour'.

23 August

Umhlanga Day in Swaziland

Good day for: *setting a record*
Bad day for: *the Roman Empire*
Hot day for: *penguins*

Records of the day include the following. In 1958, Marie Ashton finished a 133-hour piano-playing marathon to set a new women's world record; in 1960 the world's largest frog, weighing 3.3 kilograms, was caught in Equatorial Guinea; and in 1977, Bryan Ashton made the first man-powered flight over a distance greater than one mile.

This was the day in the year 410 when the Visigoths are considered to have sacked Rome, thus heralding the end of the Empire. On this day in 1617, a small sign of advancing civilisation was the introduction in London of the first one-way streets.

On 23 August 1997, Edinburgh Zoo reported that it had been using suncream on its penguins during an unprecedented spell of hot weather. The heat had caused the birds to moult more than usual, leaving patches of bare skin that needed protection from the sun.

Birth of the day: Louis XVI of France (1754).

24 August

Feast day of St Bartholomew, patron saint of shoemakers and tanners

Good day for: *a massacre*
Lucky garment: *bikini*
Chef's speciality of the day: *waffles with chips*

St Bartholomew is said to have been flayed alive, then beheaded, sometime during the first century; the St Bartholomew's Day Massacre, of thousands of French Protestants, began in Paris on this day in 1572.

Inventions of the day include the waffle-iron in 1869 and the first potato chips, deep-fried by George Crum in 1853. Bernard Castro, inventor of the convertible couch, died on this day in 1991.

Disasters of the day: in AD 79 Vesuvius erupted, burying Pompeii, Herculaneum and Stabiae; and in 1997 a rat gnawed through a cable at a hospital in northern Honduras causing a short-circuit and a blackout that caused the deaths of 13 people and one rat.

On 24 August 1946 in Newquay, Maisie Dunn became the first to wear a bikini on a UK beach; and in 1975 Annabel Hunt became the first actress to appear nude on British television—in an opera from Glyndebourne broadcast on STV.

25 August

Feast day of St Genesius, patron saint of actors

Good day for: *firsts*
Lucky adjectives: *'mad', 'terrible'*
Unlucky diseases: *appendicitis and malaria*

There is no evidence that St Genesius the actor ever existed, but St Genesius of Arles has the same feast day.

Births of the day include Ivan the Terrible (1530) and Mad King Ludwig of Bavaria (1845). Death of the day: Clara Maass, in 1901, an army nurse who sacrificed her life at the age of 25 to prove that yellow fever is carried by a mosquito.

This was the date of the first swim across the English Channel, by Matthew Webb in 1875; of the first scheduled international daily air service, from London to Paris in 1919; of the first international polo match, England versus the USA in 1886; of the first parachute wedding, in 1940; and of the first soccer tournament for robots, in Nagoya, Japan, in 1997.

Quote of the day: 'We all make mistakes'—the head of surgery at a Hong Kong hospital after removing one of a young girl's Fallopian tubes instead of her appendix in 1997.

26 August

....

Propitious academic discipline: *belly-dancing*
Unlucky vehicle: *shopping-trolley*
Lucky animal: *deer*

This is an important day in British history: in 55 BC Julius Caesar's Roman forces invaded Britain, and in 1346 the British successfully introduced the longbow into warfare to defeat the French at the Battle of Crécy. It is also an important day for America, for on this day in 1973 the University of Texas at Arlington became the first US academic institution to offer a course in belly-dancing.

On 26 August 1996, RJB Mining of Harworth started building a £10,000 noise barrier, 24 feet (7.3 metres) high, around an open-cast mine in Derbyshire to avoid disturbing nearby deer during the rutting season. In Sweden on the very same day, a drunken man became the first person to be charged with dangerous handling of a shopping-trolley. He was hurtling downhill at 30 mph when he collided with a car.

In 1997, a model of the Malaysian flag was constructed from 10,430 floppy disks—'An event Malaysia can be proud of,' said the deputy education minister.

27 August

....

Good day for: *women's breasts*
Bad day for: *men's chests*
Sad day for: *a camel*

This was the day in 1869 when a boat race from Mortlake to Putney in London between Harvard and Oxford Universities attracted a million spectators and more press coverage than any sporting event of the previous 50 years. This was also the day in 1961 when Francis the talking mule was the mystery guest on the television programme *What's My Line?*

On 27 August 1997, a camel at Knowsley Safari Park on Merseyside was killed by lightning. On the same day, the space between a woman's breasts was given a name by the International Federation of Associations of Anatomists: the intermammary sulcus. On 27 August 1996, a survey in *Bella* magazine revealed that 22 per cent of women prefer a man with body hair, while 57 per cent are disgusted by it.

Disaster of the day: in 1883, an eruption on Krakatoa blew up most of the island. The noise of the eruption was heard in Australia over 2,000 miles away, and the resulting tidal waves killed 36,000.

28 August

Festival of Hungry Ghosts in Hong Kong

Good day for: *cellular phones, bad hair and lap dancers*
Bad day for: *clay pigeons*
Lucky seeds: *lettuce*

The first radio commercial was broadcast on this day in 1922, advertising an apartment block in New York. In 1932, the Tomatina festival was first held in Buñol, Spain, when people throw tomatoes at each other—the annual event began when summer residents made fun of the town youths and were pelted with tomatoes.

On 28 August 1983, Joseph Kreckman set a new record by shooting 2,215 clay pigeons in an hour; and on this day in 1988, the Yantlee Polyclinic in Bangkok claimed that you can kill hunger by pressing lettuce seeds into your ears ten times before meals.

On 28 August 1996, in Amsterdam, a suspected mugger was arrested after being identified by a print taken from a fingertip that one of his intended victims had bitten off.

In 1997 'cellular phone', 'bad hair day' and 'lap dancer' were among the new expressions in *Webster's College Dictionary* published today.

29 August

Lucky form of transport: *motor-bike*
Chef's special: *chop-suey*
Bad day to: *foul the footpath*

On 29 August 1882, England lost to Australia at cricket for the first time. 'The Ashes' have their origin in the obituary for English cricket that subsequently appeared in the *Sporting Times*.

This was the day in 1896 when chop-suey was invented in New York—by the chef of the Chinese ambassador—as a dish that would appeal to both Americans and Chinese.

On this day in 1885 Gottfried Daimler received a patent for the first motor-cycle, and in 1909 the world's first air race was held in France.

Ingrid Bergman was born on this day in 1915, and died on her 67th birthday in 1982.

Quote of the day: 'It's a problem and we have to deal with it'—Amon Perlman, spokesman for the city of Tel Aviv, on its announcement on 29 August 1997 that it was launching squads of undercover inspectors with cameras and night-vision equipment to catch people who let their dogs foul the footpath.

30 August

Animal of the day: *rabbit*
Bad day for: *sideburns*
Labour-saving device of the day: *vacuum cleaner*

At an auction in London of Elvis Presley memorabilia on 30 August 1997, his kitbag fetched £10,350 but a lock of hair from his sideburns failed to reach its reserve price.

In 1860 on this day, Britain's first tramway system opened in Birkenhead; in 1881, the first stereo system was patented by Clement Adler of Germany; and in 1901 Herbert Cecil Booth patented the vacuum cleaner.

This is a prolific day for notable deaths: in 30 BC, Cleopatra VII (the famous one) committed suicide; in 1483, Louis XI of France died; and in 1930 William Taft, 27th president of the USA, died.

In 1963, it was the day that the 'hot line' between the White House and the Kremlin became operational, and in 1979 it was the day President Carter was attacked by a rabbit when on a canoe trip in Georgia.

Birth of the day: Mary Shelley (1797), creator of Frankenstein.

31 August

Lucky profession: *film star*
Lucky number: *33*
Lucky drink: *Coca-Cola*

In 1887 on this day, Thomas Edison patented the kinetoscope, the first device for producing moving pictures. Both James Coburn and Richard Gere, born on 31 August 1928 and 1949 respectively, were subsequently grateful for that invention.

On this day in 1900 Coca-Cola went on sale in Britain; two years later Mrs Adolph Landeburg, a horse-rider, wore the first split skirt; on 31 August 1951 Deutsche Grammophon launched the 33 rpm long-playing record; and in 1954 Hurricane Carol, which hit New England causing 70 deaths, was the first storm to be given a name.

Death of the day: Leofric, husband of Lady Godiva, in 1057. It was Leofric's unpopular tax plans that are reputed to have caused Godiva to ride naked through the streets of Coventry.

Quote of the day: 'It's basic human nature'—Dr William Fitzgerald on 31 August 1997, explaining the baby boom in Washington nine months after a string of severe winter storms.

1 September

Good day for: *lamb*
Bad day for: *pigeon*
Beware of: *penguins*

This is a good day for heavyweight boxers: both James 'Gentleman Jim' Corbett (1866) and Rocky Marciano (1923) were born on 1 September. It was also the birthday, in 1875, of Edgar Rice Burroughs, the creator of Tarzan.

Deaths of the day include that of Adrian IV, the only English Pope, in 1159; of Louis XIV of France in 1715; and of Martha, the last known passenger-pigeon in the world, at Cincinnati Zoo in 1914.

Other notable events of the day: in 1830 Sarah J. Hale published her nursery rhyme, 'Mary had a little lamb'; in 1878 in Boston, Massachusetts, Emma Nutt became the world's first female telephone operator; in 1951 Britain's first supermarket opened in Earl's Court, London; and in 1988, the New York Health Department announced that in the previous year 8,064 people had been treated in hospital after being bitten by dogs, 1,587 had been treated after being bitten by people, and one after having been bitten by a penguin.

---

2 September

Good day for: *dwarfs*
Bad day for: *pigs*
Busy day for: *prostitutes*

This day has a place in the history of the Olympics: it is said to have been the date in 490 BC when Pheidippides ran from Marathon to Athens to bring news of the Greek victory over the Persians—and then dropped dead. Baron Pierre de Coubertin, founder of the modern Olympics, also died on this day in 1937.

Three important events happened on 2 September 1997: in England, 40 pigs flew a quarter of a mile through the air after a tornado hit a farm in Sutton-on-Trent; in Mexico City, prostitutes promised not to wear skirts more than four fingers above the knee or see-through clothing before 10 p.m., and not to solicit near schools or churches; and in Hong Kong, Chan Wing-hong was found not guilty of murder and of dismembering his prostitute lover—the court accepted his plea of manslaughter when they heard that it was after she had called him a 'bloody dwarf' that he had stabbed her in the heart and scattered her body parts in rubbish bins. Mr Wing-hong is 4ft 6in (1.37 metres) tall.

---

3 September

Attractive feature of the day: *ugliness*
Good day to: *cross the road*
Unlucky year: *1752*

This day, and the next ten, did not exist in Britain in 1752. They were omitted to accomplish the change-over from the Julian to the Gregorian calendar. Another country to have reversed the status quo today is Sweden, which switched from driving on the left to driving on the right in 1967.

In English history, this was the day in 1189 that Richard the Lionheart came to the throne, and that Oliver Cromwell died, in 1658. Ho Chi Minh died today, too, in 1969.

Discovery of the day: in 1997 researchers at the Institute of Urban Ethology in Vienna found that ugly men smell more attractive than handsome men. The result came from correlating attractiveness ratings given by women to photographs of the men with ratings given to the smell of T-shirts they had been wearing for three days.

Quote of the day: 'The camel is also a reason for them to invade Libya'—Colonel Qadhafi, warning his people in 1997 to fear the West. Sand and water-melons were other potential causes for invasion.

4 September

Unlucky job: *lion-keeper*
Good day to: *go back to work*
Lucky number: *7*

Britain's first lioness died on this day in the Tower of London in 1733. A special post of Keeper of the Lion Office had been created for the man who looked after her.

Firsts of the day include the first district to be lit by Edison's light-bulbs—around Pearl Street Station in New York in 1882; the first cafeteria opening in New York City in 1885; and George Eastman's patenting of the first roll-film camera in 1888, when he took the opportunity to register the name 'Kodak' as well.

Work recommenced on Cologne Cathedral on this day in 1842, after a gap of 284 years.

The most satisfied man of the day must have been Mark Spitz, who became the first to win seven Olympic gold medals on 4 September 1972. The most dissatisfied may have been John Wayne Bobbitt, who threatened on 4 September 1997 to sue the plastic surgeon who had reattached his severed penis, claiming it was 'cock-eyed'.

5 September

National Be-Late-for-Something Day in the USA

....

Recommended vocations: *king and petrol pump attendant*
Bad day for: *ghosts*
Lucky animal: *pet dog*

This was the birthday of both Louis VIII of France (1187) and Louis XIV (1638). It was also the day in 1995 when Prince Bhekimpi of Swaziland announced his determination to ban ghosts from the Enkhaba region, where they had been terrorising people in their homes by stealing blankets and ordering them to cook food.

In 1885, it was the day when the first petrol pump was delivered to a garage-owner in Indiana.

Human rights issue of the day: in 1997 staff of AT&T in Wellington, New Zealand, won the right to take 'dog days' off work in order to look after sick pets.

Quote of the day: 'If you're not in the habit of procrastinating, this might be the one day to just try it out'—Les Waas, founder of the Procrastinators' Club of America, launching National Be-Late-for-Something Day in 1997.

6 September

....

Favourite television programme: Star Trek
Lucky food: *chapati with evaporated milk*
Unlucky body part: *ear*

Forty-one thousand Parisians had a startling experience on 6 September 1989 when a computer error led to their being sent letters charging them with murder, extortion and organised prostitution instead of parking offences.

Gastronomic delights of the day: in 1899, Carnation processed its first can of evaporated milk; in 1987, military scientists in India announced the first long-life chapati.

Great British firsts on this day include the first free lending library, opened in 1852 in Manchester; the first telephone exchange, opened in London in 1879; and the first home cricket test match against Australia, which began on 6 September 1880.

The first broadcast of *Star Trek* was on this day in 1966, and in 1994 Saddam Hussein added ear amputation and tattooing to the list of possible penalties for convicted criminals in Iraq.

Death of the day: Suleiman the Magnificent, in 1566.

7 September

Bad day for: *clay pigeons*
Lucky accessory: *belt*
Lucky mode of transport: *Ark*

According to the theologian Gustav Seyffarth, this was the date in 3446 BC when the Great Flood came to an end.

Other notable historical events of the day include the following:

1880: George Ligowsky patented a device to launch clay pigeons for people to shoot at.

1908: botany professor Harold Wager claimed that plants have eyes and can see.

1914: James van Allen, discoverer of radiation belts now known as 'van Allen belts', was born.

1921: Margaret Gorman, a 15-year-old blonde from Washington, became the first Miss America.

1973: the crew of a Royal Navy frigate were accused of throwing carrots at an Icelandic gunboat.

1996: a survey revealed that 73 per cent of British dog-owners had taken time off work because their pet was sick.

8 September

Recommended profession: *Goon*
Lucky accessory: *codpiece*
Good day for: *fooling people*

Two members of the *Goon Show* have shared this birthday: Harry Secombe (1921) and Peter Sellers (1925). A third comedian born on this day was Sid Caesar (1922).

In 1974, this was the day when one man was forgiven for trying to fool all of the people: ex-President Richard Nixon was pardoned by his successor, Gerald Ford, for any federal crimes that he might have committed. Another disaster for America happened on 8 September 1900 when the most deadly hurricane in the country's history destroyed Galveston, Texas, killing 6,000 people.

Sartorial innovation of the day: the première of the musical *Blondel* by Tim Rice and Stephen Oliver in 1983 saw the first public appearance of a denim codpiece.

Quote of the day: 'You can fool all of the people some of the time, and some of the people all of the time, but you cannot fool all of the people all of the time'—Abraham Lincoln in a speech at Clinton on 8 September 1858.

9 September

Recommended vocation: *bodyguard*
Unlucky organ: *ear*
Bad day for: *hackers*

On this day in 1997, a Cincinnati woman was put on probation for child neglect after letting her children live in squalor while she spent up to 12 hours a day on the Internet. Her name was Hacker. On the same day, a Spaniard was sentenced to four years in gaol for a series of robberies in Geneva. He had been tracked down by the earprints he left on doors.

On 9 September 1995, the World Association of Bodyguards meeting in Budapest attracted 130 delegates from 40 countries.

Birth of the day: William Bligh, captain of the *Bounty* (1754).

Deaths: William the Conqueror (1087), Mao Zedong (1976).

Quote of the day: 'I'm not trying to spoil anybody's fun but I would urge customers to keep their trousers on at all times'—Jim Hornsby of North Tyneside Council on 9 September 1997, when he renewed the licence for Idols topless bar in Whitley Bay but insisted that tighter controls on noise and behaviour would be needed.

10 September

Good day for: *hypnotists*
Bad day for: *toothache sufferers*
Beware of: *meteorites*

A 48-kilogram meteorite fell on the town of Adare in Ireland on this day in 1813. In 1897 George Smith, a London taxi-driver, became the first person to be convicted of drunken driving. He was fined £1. And in 1995 Ismail Ayyildiz, 33, died in hospital in Turkey from head wounds after he had attempted to shoot out a bad tooth.

Two labour-saving devices were introduced on this day: in 1846, Elias Howe patented his sewing-machine, and in 1869 the rickshaw was invented in Yokohama, Japan.

Other notable events: on 10 September 1987, Westminster Council lifted a 35-year ban on stage hypnotists; and in 1995 a survey showed that one in three British children believe that their mum prefers the cat to dad.

Quote of the day: 'We did make inquiries, and a person who fits the description of the loser was seen at about 3.30, possibly confused, looking for the leg'—a spokesman for Stamford police, seeking the owner of an artificial leg in 1996.

11 September

Good day for: *pregnant brides*
Bad day for: *country life*
Suicidal day for: *country music*

In 1905 on this day, the British government blamed an increase in lunacy on the tedium of country life; and in 1996, psychologists at Loughborough University reported that the suicide rate among white urban males in certain areas of the USA correlated with the frequency of country music played on the radio.

Artistic event of the day: in 1996, Jane Sanders' one-woman show *England's Glory* had its first night during the interval at the Gulbenkian Studio Theatre in Newcastle-upon-Tyne in both the ladies and the gentlemen's lavatories.

Fashion event of the day: in 1995, the first white wedding dress for pregnant brides was launched at the bridal fair in Harrogate.

Births of the day: writer D. H. Lawrence (1885), and Philippines dictator Ferdinand Marcos (1917).

Death of the day: Georgi Markov (1978), stabbed in London with the poisoned tip of a Bulgarian umbrella.

12 September

Good day for: *a wedding*
Bad day for: *obedience*
Lucky day for: *pigs*

Both Winston Churchill (in 1908) and John F. Kennedy (in 1953) got married on this day. Kennedy may not have known that this was also the day in 1922 when the House of Bishops of the US Episcopal Church voted to delete the word 'obey' from the marriage vows.

On 12 September 1379 Philip the Bold, Duke of Burgundy, pardoned two herds of swine that had been condemned to death as accomplices to the killing of an infant by a sow.

Other significant events: in 1910 on this day, Alice Wells of the Los Angeles Police Department became America's first policewoman; in 1960 MOT tests for cars were introduced in Britain.

Death of the day: Hopalong Cassidy (William Boyd) in 1972.

Quote of the day: 'It was obvious after a few trains ran over her that she was dead'—a spokesman for the Sydney ambulance service in 1997 after rail officials had apologised for keeping rush-hour trains running over the body of a woman who had committed suicide.

13 September

Dante Alighieri Day

....

Good day to: *build a wall*
Procreative day for: *the Beatles*
Favourite pet: *goat*

This was the day in AD 122 when building began on Hadrian's Wall. On the same day in 1788 New York became the federal capital of the United States.

On 13 September 1902, Harry Jackson became the first person in Britain to be convicted on the basis of fingerprint evidence, and in 1922 El Aziz in Libya registered the hottest temperature ever recorded: 58°C (136.4°F). In 1996, the *Zimbabwe Independent* newspaper accused Vice-President Joshua Nkomo of rearing more than 100 goats at his official residence.

Births of the day: Zak Starkey (1965), son of Beatle Ringo, and Stella Nina McCartney (1971), daughter of Beatle Paul.

Quote of the day: 'As a playwright, I am an expert on sex appeal'— George Bernard Shaw talking at the Congress for Sexual Reform in 1929.

---

14 September

....

Good day for: *typing*
Bad day for: *car journeys*
Lucky profession: *assassin*

Two assassinations happened on this day: President William McKinley in 1901 and Pyotr Stolypin, prime minister of Russia, in 1911. Other deaths today include Henry Bliss (1899), the first American automobile fatality; Isadora Duncan (1927), who was strangled by her scarf when it became entangled in her steering-wheel; and Princess Grace of Monaco (1982), killed in a car crash.

More happily, 14 September 1868 saw the first recorded hole-in-one at golf, scored by Tom Morris at Prestwick, and in 1891 the first penalty kick in English league football.

Innovations of the day: the typewriter ribbon, patented in 1886 by George Anderson; and the first prefrontal lobotomy was performed in Washington in 1956.

Achievement of the day: in 1997 Jade Kindar-Martin and Didier Pasquette became the first to cross the River Thames simultaneously, starting from opposite ends of the same tightrope.

---

15 September

Good day for: *poor taste*
Bad day for: *a train journey*
Socially acceptable day for: *infidelity*

In 1965 on this day, British prime minister Harold Wilson admitted that he liked the soap opera *Coronation Street*. In 1997, the Pizza Express chain showed slightly better taste when they dropped plans for a Diana Pizza in memory of the late princess. The pizza was to have included leeks as a symbol of Wales.

Political assassination of the day: in 1996 police in Brazil were reported to be investigating the suspicious death of a goat which had been standing as a protest candidate for the post of mayor of a small town. The goat's owner suspected he had been poisoned.

In 1830 on this day William Huskisson, President of the Board of Trade, became the first railway fatality as he stepped in front of Stephenson's *Rocket* at the opening of the Liverpool and Manchester Railway.

On 15 September 1997, a poll showed that 26 per cent of Canadians view infidelity as socially acceptable, while 51 per cent thought it more socially acceptable than it had been ten years before.

16 September

Good day for: *bright male guppies*
Bad day for: *snogging in the back row*
Furious day for: *owners of lilac or lime-coloured cars*

On this day in 1996, researchers at the University of New Brunswick published their finding that female guppy fish prefer brightly coloured males to drab ones. Exactly one year later, research carried out by the RAC showed that owners of pastel-coloured cars were eight times more likely to suffer from depression than people with bright-coloured cars. Drivers of lilac and lime cars were the most likely to suffer from road rage.

On 16 September 1997, the state of Kelantan in Malaysia announced that lights would be kept on in cinemas to prevent kissing and cuddling. 'If we can watch television at home with the lights on, then why not in cinemas?' chief minister Nik Aziz Nik Mat asked.

Song of the day: 'Jingle Bells', registered by Jane Pierpoint in 1857 under the name 'One Horse Open Sleigh'.

Feat of the day: the world's biggest liver dumpling, weighing 1.8 tonnes, was cooked in the Austrian village of Zams in 1996.

17 September

Vegetable of the day: *cucumber*
Meat of the day: *chicken legs*
Good day for: *swearing*

In Fort Lauderdale, Florida, on 17 September 1997 a woman was arrested after allegedly throwing frozen chicken legs, a telephone and a circular saw at her boyfriend when he came home late. She was charged with aggravated battery and throwing a deadly missile.

On the very same day, researchers in Britain threw 500 cucumbers into the Irish Sea in order to find out why sheep droppings were being washed up on English beaches. The cucumbers were painted five different colours for identification purposes and had been chosen because they float just below the surface and are driven by tides.

News in brief: on this day in 1910 a London doctor warned that if lunacy continued to increase at the same rate, the insane would outnumber the sane by 1950; in 1996 a researcher at the University of Florida revealed that swearing may relieve stress; and also in 1996 the Kedah state government in Malaysia proposed giving children crew cuts to make them easier to identify when they skip classes.

18 September

Good day for: *wife-beating*
Disease of the day: *leprosy*
Meal of the day: *pizza*

On this day in 1996, Italy's highest appeal court overturned the conviction of a man for wife-beating, because he only beat her from time to time. Occasional bouts of wife-beating were ruled to be legal. A year later, a Belgian study showed that couples in which both partners work argue more than couples with only one breadwinner.

On 18 September 1997, the authorities in Bangkok offered rewards for people who bring lepers to hospital for treatment: 250 *baht* (about £4) for early stages of the disease, and 500 *baht* for chronic cases.

Record of the day: in 1995, a 200-metre long pizza was cooked in Malo, Italy. Crime of the day: also in 1995, a motorist in Carlisle was fined £140 for throwing a doughnut at a traffic warden.

Quote of the day: 'A survey showed that women civil servants don't like sporting metaphors, so perhaps we will have to ban level playing fields, own goals and that sort of thing'—Sir Terry Burns, Treasury civil servant, on 18 September 1995.

19 September

Feast day of St Gennaro (Januarius)

Recommended profession: *witch-sniffer*
Good day for: *women's rights*
Good day for: *male libido*

There is a vial in Naples Cathedral containing a powdery substance alleged to be the blood of St Gennaro. Each year on 19 September and on the first Saturday in May the vial is put on display. If it does not liquefy, it is said to be an omen of disaster. It failed to liquefy in 1527, when 40,000 people died of plague, and in 1980 when 3,000 were killed by an earthquake in southern Italy.

On this day in 1888, the world's first beauty contest was held in Belgium; in 1893 New Zealand became the first country to give women the vote; in 1997, education authorities in South Africa said that although they disapproved of two schools arranging witch-sniffing ceremonies to root out teacher sorcerers, they could do nothing to stop them.

Quote of the day: 'There needs to be plenty of air around the vital parts for healthy sperm and testosterone production, and testicles must be allowed to hang freely'—advice from the Well Man clinic in London in 1997 against tightly fitting underpants made of synthetic fibres.

20 September

Good day for: *socialist morality and hot drinks*
Bad day for: *John Major*
Narrow escape for: *cats*

This was the day in 1996 when a police dog trod in a cake that had been prepared for John Major at a children's club in Huntingdon. Exactly a year later, another eating experience was spoiled when the Great Gastronomic Kitty Festival of cat cookery in Cañete, Chile, was cancelled after complaints from animal rights groups. A spokesperson for the Association of Animal Friends said: 'We have saved the cats' lives. The cat is not an animal for domestic consumption; it can transmit diseases like toxoplasmosis.'

Births of the day: James Dewar (1842), inventor of the vacuum flask; Sophia Loren (1934), actress.

On 20 September 1996 officials in Chengdu, China, banned the sale of 'Opium' perfume by Yves St Laurent, because its name undermined socialist morality. On the same date in 1959, Soviet premier Nikita Khrushchev had his request to visit Disneyland in America turned down. It was considered to be too great a security risk.

21 September

National day of Malta

....

Important day for: *literature*
Excellent day for: *astrology*
Bad day for: *the royal family*

It was on 21 September 1986 that Prince Charles admitted on television that he talks to his plants, and exactly a year later his cousin Viscount Linley became the first member of the royal family to be banned from driving.

The Italian mathematician, astrologer, physician and charlatan Giro-lamo Cardano successfully predicted his own death on this day in 1576. He woke up feeling fine, but the prediction came true later in the day when he killed himself.

Many notable events connected with books have happened today. It saw the birth, in 1902, of Allen Lane, who went on to found Penguin Books. It is also the birthday of H. G. Wells (1866) and of Stephen King (1947), and the day of the deaths of Sir Walter Scott (1832) and of Virgil (19 BC). Most notable of all, it was the day in 1937 when J. R. R. Tolkien published *The Hobbit*.

22 September

....

Good day for: *football managers*
Musical day for: *hens*
Lucky number: *10*

Research of the day: in 1997, a survey published in the *Journal of the Institute of Economic Affairs* showed that soccer clubs do not benefit from sacking their managers. In Israel on the same day, Esther and Yossi Dvir reported that hens at their farm in Kfar Hess had been laying more eggs since they started playing classical music to them.

This was the day in 1735 when Sir Robert Walpole became the first prime minister to occupy number 10 Downing Street. In 1920, the Metro-politan Police 'Flying Squad' was formed, and in 1955 the first television advertisement in Britain advised viewers to brush their teeth with Gibbs SR toothpaste.

It has been a good day for electricity: in 1791 Michael Faraday was born, and in 1888 delegates to the Electrical Conference in Paris agreed on the terms 'ampere', 'volt' and 'ohm'.

Death of the day: Huan Huan, in 1997 at the age of 25—the only giant panda ever to have given birth in Japan.

23 September

Your lucky planet: *Neptune*
Your lucky confectionery: *chewing-gum*
Your recommended profession: *undertaker or tramp*

In 1846 on this day, Johann Galle discovered Neptune; in 1848 John Curtis produced the first commercially available chewing-gum, which he called State of Maine Pure Spruce Gum; and in 1897 on this day a nine-year-old boy in Hackney, London, became the first motor-car casualty on a public highway. Exactly 100 years after that death, the American Board of Funeral Service Education reported a record level of students enrolling on mortuary science programmes.

On 23 September 1996 the first world conference of the Free Tramps' Movement began in Mar del Plata in Argentina.

Death of the day: Sigmund Freud (1939).

Quote of the day: 'It is a method used in the Stone Age in Sweden . . . the smell disappears when you rinse the skins in water'—Swedish artist Ann-Kristin Antman in 1996, presenting her design of an anorak made from salmon skins soaked in human urine.

24 September

Good day for: *killing rats*
Bad day for: *going to the pictures*
Animal of the day: *aardvark*

On this day in 1916, that wise American naturalist John Burroughs warned that moving pictures deprive people of brain power. In 1928, however, Sir Oswald Mosley clearly still had his brains intact: when challenged over whether his title was compatible with being a Labour MP, he said that the title didn't mean anything and therefore was not worth giving up.

On 24 September 1967, the first aardvark to be born in captivity in the West weighed in at 4lb 2oz in a zoo in Miami; and in 1997 Bangladesh launched a campaign with the target of killing 3.5 million rats. Rewards of radios and televisions were offered to those who could produce the most rat tails.

Meanwhile in Northern Ireland, 24 September 1997 saw a court in Belfast trying the case of a man who had turned himself in after seeing pictures of himself robbing a garage on television. He had been too drunk at the time to remember committing the crime.

25 September

Recommended profession: *musician*
Unlucky clothing: *blue jeans*
Good day to: *sweep the carpet*

Births of the day: Jean-Philippe Rameau (1683), French composer of keyboard works and operas; Dmitri Shostakovich (1906), Russian composer of symphonies, operas, chamber works, film music and everything else; and Sir Colin Davis (1927), British conductor. Another birth of the day: Melvyn Reuben Bissell (1843), inventor of the carpet-sweeper.

Funeral of the day: 1769—Honoretta Pratt, whose cremation was the first to be recorded in Britain.

On this day in 1818, Guy's Hospital in London was the first to use human blood for a transfusion, and in 1997 about 1,200 postmen were suspended without pay by Canada's federal postal service because they had come to work wearing blue jeans as a protest at the slow progress being made in their pay talks.

Survey of the day: in 1995, research showed that 38 per cent of Canadian women prefer eating chocolate to making love.

26 September

Good day for: *26 per cent of elderly French people*
Unlucky profession: *rickshaw-driver*
Dish of the day: *fish fingers*

Gastronomic news: in 1953 sugar rationing came to an end in Britain, and in 1955 Birds Eye fish fingers first went on sale.

Traffic news: on this day in 1997, the Indian state of West Bengal announced that rickshaws would be banned in Calcutta because they are slow and disrupt traffic.

Invention of the day: in 1887, Emile Berliner was granted a patent for his gramophone, an improvement on Thomas Edison's earlier sound-recording devices.

Survey of the day: in 1995 it was revealed that 26 per cent of French people over the age of 60 make love at least once a week.

Rarity of the day: in 1950 a blue moon, caused by freak atmospheric conditions, was visible over south-east England.

Assassinations of the day: Hirobumi Ito, four times prime minister of Japan (1909), shot by a Korean revolutionary; Solomon Bandaranaike (1959), prime minister of Ceylon, shot by a Buddhist monk.

27 September

Good day for: *names*
Stressful day for: *koalas*
Confusing day for: *transsexuals*

Nicknames: this was the day in 1888 when the name 'Jack the Ripper' was coined—in a letter to the Central News Agency.

First names: on this day in 1995 the annual 'BobFest' in Avon, Colorado, for people named Bob was cancelled. Tom Britz, founder and organiser of the event, announced that he was tired of running it. 'I met one bad Bob and it spoiled the bunch,' he said.

Surnames: on 27 September 1995, the Supreme Court in South Korea ruled that marriages between people with the same last name are legal if they have first been married abroad. On the same day, South Korean judges said they were unsure whether rape charges could be filed against two men who raped a transsexual. The accused had appealed for mercy, saying that they thought the victim, a Mr Gil, was a woman.

Today in 1995, Japanese firms began cancelling tours to Australia after a ban was imposed on cuddling koalas because the animals find cuddling stressful.

28 September

Feast day of St Wenceslas

Song of the day: *'God Save the King'*
Shop of the day: *Marks & Spencer*
Lucky animal: *tortoise*

The 'Good King Wenceslas' celebrated in the well known carol by J. M. Neale was a prince of Bohemia who tried to lead his country towards Christianity but was killed by his pagan brother Boleslav in 929. The feast of Stephen is 26 December. The poem is pure fiction.

The British national anthem, 'God Save the King', was first sung in public on this day in 1745 at the Drury Lane Theatre in London. Another great British tradition began in 1894, when Michael Marks and Thomas Spencer opened their first Penny Bazaar in Manchester. Exactly ten years later, a woman was arrested for smoking on 5th Avenue in New York.

On 28 September 1995 in the village of Lyde, near Hereford, Malcolm Edwards was surprised when his pet tortoise Chester was spotted walking down a path not far from his home. It had been missing for 35 years.

29 September

Good day for: *shoe salesmen*
Bad day for: *the Addams family*
Athletic day for: *transplant recipients*

This was the historic day at the United Nations Assembly in 1960 when Nikita Khrushchev thumped the table with a shoe as British prime minister Harold Macmillan was speaking. Television pictures clearly showed the Russian leader was still wearing two shoes at the time. Macmillan asked for the shoe-banging to be translated.

The 1997 World Transplant Games began in Sydney on this day with 150 entrants, all transplant recipients, from 51 nations.

This is a good day for the birth of heroes: Pompey the Great (106 BC), (Robert) Clive of India (1725), Horatio Nelson (1758) and Lech Wałęsa (1943).

Death of the day: Charles Addams (1988), ghoulish American cartoonist.

Quote of the day: 'I'm sure Jimmy would have wanted us to do that. He would have done the same'—a golfer at a club in Fife in 1996, who played on with three regular partners after a fourth, Jimmy Hogg, 77, had dropped dead at the first tee.

30 September

Good day for: *opera*
Bad day for: *racial equality*
Lucky day for: *leg fetishists*

Both Mozart's *Magic Flute* and Gershwin's *Porgy and Bess* received their first performances on this day, in 1791 and 1935 respectively.

In 1906 on this day Paris staged the world's first hot-air balloon race, and in 1947 the British government told women that it would be in the national interest for them to save cloth by avoiding the fashion for longer skirts.

Events of 30 September 1997: in the Ukraine, an opinion poll revealed in the run-up to an election that one third of voters would sell their votes to the highest bidders—suggested prices ranged from about £7 to £250. In Australia, the Myer group of stores applied to the Anti-discrimination Tribunal in Melbourne for a waiver to allow them to advertise for white male Santa Clauses.

Quote of the day: 'I believe it is peace in our time'—Neville Chamberlain in 1938.

1 October

Recommended profession: *taxi-driver*
Bad day for: *cosmetics*
Good day for: *a minor accident*

This was the day in 1928 when Elastoplast dressings were first manufactured. They would have been of no use to Lady Coventry, who died on 1 October 1760 after painting her face with white lead, thus making her the first modern martyr to cosmetics.

Other firsts of the day include the opening of Disneyworld in Florida in 1971 and the first McDonald's in London in 1974.

On 1 October 1995, Leeds University shelved plans to run a course on the works of Catherine Cookson, because nobody had signed up for it. Exactly two years later, the state of Tabasco in Mexico banned the sale of cold beer as part of a drive to curtail alcoholism.

On this day in 1996 Klaus Bettel, a psychologist for the Danish cab-drivers' union, said that research had shown that some 50 per cent of the country's young male taxi-drivers had been offered sex by female passengers.

2 October

Good day for: *prayer*
Witty day for: *forgery*
Lucky food: *porridge*

This was the birthday of both Mohandas K. Gandhi (1869), the founder of independent India, and Shri Lal Bahadur Shastri (1904), who became its prime minister in 1964. 2 October 1996 was celebrated as the 21st birthday of Batchelor's mushy peas, and on the very same day Professor Bryan Clarke of Nottingham University was reported to have saved a species of rare snail by feeding it porridge.

A Spaniard, Eduardo Sierra, was reported on 2 October 1996 to have become a millionaire thanks to his having stopped at a Catholic church in Sweden and prayed for the remains of an unknown man lying in a coffin. He later learnt that the man had left all his belongings 'to whoever prays for my soul first'.

On this day in 1997, Czech police found an 'exceptionally well forged' 1,000-crown note in the town of Jablonec. All that gave it away was that the words 'Forging of notes will be prosecuted in accordance with the law' had been replaced by 'This note is a fake.'

3 October

Good day for: *pregnant soldiers*
Mad day for: *cats*
Unlucky number: *38*

On 3 October 1995, the British Ministry of Defence announced its first contract for maternity uniforms. 'Pregnant ladies said they wanted to stay identified with the service as long as possible,' a spokesman commented.

On the same day, Kiev council established a commission to rename 38 streets in the city that had been causing confusion: they were all called 'Vostochnaya' (East).

Inventions of the day: in 1899, the first motor-driven vacuum cleaner was patented by J. S. Thurman; and in 1941 the aerosol was patented by L. Goodhue and W. Sullivan.

Other major events: on this day in 1906, SOS replaced CDQ as the international distress signal; in 1921 Berlin waiters began refusing tips as part of a demand for better wages; and in 1996 the first case was reported of feline spongiform encephalopathy (mad cat disease) in Liechtenstein.

4 October

Bad day for: *yodelling*
Fishy day for: *bar-codes*
Lucky form of transport: *escalator*

In 1988, this was the day that the Bavarian Minister for the Environment, Alfred Dick, asked people not to yodel in the Alps because it might frighten the chamois and the golden eagle.

On 4 October 1995, scientists announced the discovery that salmon have delicate markings on their ear-bones that distinguish wild salmon from farmed salmon. These markings were christened 'bar-codes', and ways were found for each hatchery to develop its own distinctive pattern.

Britain's first escalator was turned on at Earl's Court Underground station on this day in 1911; and in 1950 three generations of the Bowler family celebrated the centenary of the bowler hat.

Quote of the day: 'I don't think it's got a lot of value now'—Rex Dawkins of Wellington, New Zealand, in 1995 after the verdict in the O. J. Simpson trial was announced. Before the trial he had bought the car number plate 'OJGILT' for NZ$440 (£180), as an investment.

5 October

Good day for: *promiscuous kangaroos*
Bad day for: *breaking into a fireworks factory*
Lucky profession: *president*

This was the date of birth of both Chester Arthur (1830), who became 21st president of the USA in 1881, and Vaclav Havel (1936), who became president of Czechoslovakia in 1989.

Crime of the day: in 1995, a gang trying to break into a fireworks factory in Kent set their van on fire with their oxyacetylene torch. The blaze ignited tons of fireworks, demolishing the building. The robbers were dubbed by police 'the hole-in-the-ground gang'.

On the very same day in Australia, the Co-operative Research Centre for the Conservation and Management of Marsupials said that they hoped to have developed a kangaroo contraceptive within five years.

Wedding of the day: in 1996 Phet and Ploy, two 'diamond-eye' cats in Bangkok, celebrated an £18,000 wedding with gold rings specially made for paws. Diamond-eye is a form of glaucoma that results in a thick blue film over the lens and is believed in Thailand to bring luck. It had left each cat blind in one eye.

6 October

Recommended profession: *cricket captain*
Hellish day for: *monkeys*
Good day for: *infidelity*

According to a survey conducted among the guests at the Woman of the Year awards in London on this day in 1997, 42 per cent of top women admitted to having had an affair, and of those, 64 per cent said they had never regretted it.

6 October 1995, though, marked the first surgical sterilisation of monkeys at Hell Valley Monkey Park in Osaka, Japan. The population had got out of hand and monkeys were frequently hopping over the walls to raid nearby orchards.

Births of the day include Australian cricket captain Richie Benaud (1930) and English cricket captain Tony Greig (1946).

In 1941 on this day, two men called Willburn and Frizzel were sent to the electric chair in Florida.

Quote of the day: 'They got a shock all right'—a police spokesman in Cairns, Australia in 1996, after two men had turned themselves in after finding a dead body on the back seat of a car they had stolen.

7 October

Good day for: *starting things*
Lucky award: *Nobel prize*
Unlucky profession: *copyist*

This was the date in 1922 of the first royal broadcast on the BBC (made by the Prince of Wales), in 1950 of the first *Frank Sinatra Show* on American television, in 1982 of the opening of *Cats* on Broadway, and in 1986 of the first publication of the *Independent* newspaper in Britain.

Births of the day: Niels Bohr (1885), winner of the 1922 Nobel Prize for Physics, and Desmond Tutu (1931), winner of the 1984 Nobel Peace Prize. On the other hand, it's also a good day for losing, as Georgia Tech found in 1916 when their American football team was beaten by a record score of 222–0 by Cumberland College.

On 7 October 1806, carbon paper was patented by Ralph Wedgewood of London—spelling the end of the copyist's profession.

Quote of the day: 'There is no Soviet domination of Eastern Europe and there never will be under a Ford administration'—Gerald Ford, on 7 October 1976.

8 October

Good day for: *charity*
Bad day for: *drunken drivers*
Unlucky practice: *murder*

The first British street collection for charity took place on this day in 1891, in Manchester and Salford in aid of Lifeboat Day. On 8 October 1967, the breathalyser was first used in Britain.

Confusion of the day: in 1997, a court in Ontario sentenced a man to 12½ years for attempted murder. A month earlier, Howard Burke had been released because the foreman of the jury had coughed before saying 'Guilty' and the judge had misheard it as 'Not guilty'. After a week-long enquiry, the judge agreed an error had been made and changed the verdict. Burke's lawyer said he would appeal.

In Texas on this day in 1997 Ricky Green's last meal, before his execution by lethal injection, was five scrambled eggs, four sausage patties, eight slices of toast, six bacon rashers and four pints of milk.

In Kuwait on 8 October 1995, a man convicted of killing his sister-in-law said he shot her because she had made his wife ill by witchcraft. The defence had argued that Islamic law allows the killing of witches.

9 October

Lucky profession: *gondolier*
Unlucky profession: *witch-doctor*
Lucky part of the body: *G-spot*

'Prozac', 'G-spot' and 'road rage' were among the new entries included in the *Oxford Dictionary of New Words* published on this date in 1997. On the same day, women serving at the Dutch naval base at Willemsdorp were ordered to draw their curtains when undressing because some foreign sailors complained they had been distracted and offended.

On 9 October 1996, the waterway code in Venice was amended to allow gondoliers to serenade their customers during the day as well as in the evening and night-time. On 9 October 1997, Peruvian witch-doctors cast spells to bring misfortune to the Chilean football team in the crucial World Cup qualifier between the two countries. However, history records that Chile qualified and Peru didn't.

On this day in 1996, officials on the island of Lombok, Indonesia, announced plans to promote marital fidelity by banning wives from using contraceptives when their husbands are working overseas.

10 October

Lucky garment: *dinner-jacket*
Bad day for: *fitness*
Beware of: *caterpillars*

10 October 1886 was the date of the first appearance of a dinner-jacket—at Tuxedo Park Country Club in New York, which accounts for the American name for the garment.

According to a letter published in the *Lancet* on this day in 1996, caterpillars can be more deadly than snakes in some parts of Brazil; the poisonous hairs of the Lonomia caterpillar have three to six times the fatality rate of snakebites. On the same day, a 64-year-old man in Japan fell victim to another fatal activity: he died of a heart attack during a tug-of-war held to mark National Fitness Day.

Also on 10 October 1996, a Scottish fisherman called John Forman set a new record by finding an 82-year-old bottle with a message in it. It had been thrown into the North Sea in 1914 as part of an experiment to chart currents.

Deaths of the day include: Sir Ralph Richardson (1983), Orson Welles and Yul Brynner (both 1985).

11 October

Good day for: *eating fossilised mushrooms in the bath*
Embarrassing day for: *sleepwalking*
Dangerous sport of the day: *kite-flying*

This was the day in 1399 when the order of the Bath was constituted, and in 1919 when the first airline meals were served, on a flight from London to Paris. They were packed lunches costing three shillings each.

Some more recent events of 11 October:

1995: in New Jersey, a piece of amber 90 million years old was found with the earliest-known mushrooms embedded in it. And in Sri Lanka, air traffic controllers reported that the threat to jumbo jets from children's kites was now a thing of the past. Previously, officials and police had visited villages on the flight path to explain that kites were obstructing the approach to Colombo Airport.

1996: the Japanese company Matsushita announced the development of the first lap-top computer to withstand being dropped from a height of 70 centimetres or having coffee spilt on it. Meanwhile, in Denmark, police covered up a naked man sleepwalking in the streets of Århus and advised him to wear pyjamas in future.

12 October

Columbus Day in Spain

Good day to: *escape from a crocodile*
Bad day to: *invent the safety-pin*
Lucky shoe size: *37*

On this day in 1849 Charles Rowley patented the safety-pin in the UK, unaware that Walter Hunt had done so in the United States six months earlier.

In Rimini on 12 October 1995 Claudia Zenella, 48, was acquitted of shoplifting charges after her foot (size 37) failed to fit a shoe (size 39) left by the fleeing thief at the scene of the crime. On the same day in Australia, police saved the life of another fleeing suspect: they fired on a crocodile seen entering a river as Raymond Rankin was wading through it to escape. The crocodile swam away; Rankin reached the bank and ran off.

Other notable events of the day: in 1609, 'Three blind mice' was published in London; in 1961, the death penalty was abolished in New Zealand; in 1986 Queen Elizabeth II became the first British monarch to visit China.

13 October

Lucky profession: *mime artist*
Accent of the day: *South African*
Good day for: *plastic flamingo salesmen*

On 13 October 1996, authorities in Bogotá announced a new plan to deal with jay-walkers: they would be hauled to the side of the road and ridiculed by mime artists. On the same day, readers of the *Clothes Show* magazine voted John Major the person they would least like to see in his underpants. And in Oman Bint Hamloul, the fastest racing camel in the country, was sold for a record $390,000.

On this day in 1997, South Florida water management district announced the purchase of 108 plastic flamingos which they intended to paint white and set up in their marshlands, hoping they would attract snowy egrets, white ibis and wood storks to nest there.

On the same day, a case was reported in London of an Edinburgh woman who had suffered a minor stroke that left her speaking with a South African accent. This was only the 13th case of foreign accent syndrome ever recorded.

The cornerstone of the White House was laid this day in 1792.

14 October

Sport of the day: *soccer*
Unlucky animal: *stegosaurus*
Favourite entertainment of the day: Monty Python's *dead-parrot sketch*

In 1878 on this day, the first floodlit football match was played at Bramall Lane, Sheffield; and in 1922 the final turf was laid at Wembley Stadium.

Crime of the day: in 1996 the world's only known stegosaurus footprint was reported to have been stolen from aboriginal land north of Broome, Western Australia. In 1997, a Swedish woman was reported to be taking her local pet shop to court over a parrot which had dropped dead a couple of days after she bought it. After burying it she went to the shop to complain, but they suggested it might just have been sleeping.

Quote of the day: 'I have to admit that nine times out of ten I would rather watch the Reds than have sex. But that's no disrespect to Emma'—Kevin Morgan of Leamington Spa, after his wife had cited 'obsession with football and Manchester United' in divorce proceedings in 1997.

15 October

Bad day for: *drunken driving*
Lucky garment: *waistcoat*
Unlucky fruit: *melon*

According to Samuel Pepys, when Charles II donned a waistcoat on this day in 1666, it was the first recorded instance of anyone wearing one. History does not record whether Prince Albert was wearing a waistcoat on this day in 1839—the day Queen Victoria proposed to him.

On 15 October 1995, Norman Newmarch drove to a police station in Toronto to ask whether he was too drunk to drive home. They decided he was, and promptly charged him with drunken driving.

On this day in 1996, a British tourist in Cyprus fell to his death from a second-storey balcony. He overbalanced while trying to demonstrate his skills in throwing a melon into a municipal rubbish container.

Quote of the day: 'If I only heard from the living, I wouldn't get a very good balance'—Philip Adongo of Ghana, who had used mediums to interview village ancestors, presenting his research on ideal family sizes to a population control conference in China in 1997.

16 October

Good day for: *sweaty feet*
Lazy day for: *watch-owners*
Lucky colour: *brown*

This is a fine day for scientific advance. In 1996 researchers in Northamptonshire announced the development of the artificial sweating foot, to aid shoe manufacturers, and in 1997 researchers at Bristol University discovered why dirt is brown: their analyses of crops found in an Egyptian tomb confirmed that the formation of soil involves a chemical reaction known to produce dark-brown.

On this day in 1923 in Switzerland, John Harwood patented the self-winding watch, and in 1931 divorce was legalised in Spain.

The first Borstal school for juvenile offenders opened in the village of Borstal, Kent, on 16 October 1902, and in 1916 the first birth control clinic opened in the United States.

Births of the day: Oscar Wilde (1854), Max Bygraves (1922).

Death of the day: Marie Antoinette, at the guillotine in 1793.

Quote of the day: 'Malraux should have won it'—Albert Camus in 1957 when told he had won the Nobel Prize for Literature.

17 October

Good day to: *drive to a golf tournament in a Cadillac*
Bad day to: *argue with neighbours*
Exciting day to: *phone the Mexican Ministry of Tourism*

The first professional golf championship was held on this day in 1860 at Prestwick in Scotland, and in 1902 the first Cadillac was made in Detroit.

On 17 October 1995, a father and son were sentenced to a week's imprisonment by a Dutch court under an old law that compelled passers-by to come to the aid of a dying person. They had been having an argument with a neighbour when he collapsed of a heart attack. The law had last been invoked in 1926.

On 17 October 1997, a telephone company in Phoenix, Arizona, was embarrassed to find an out-of-date number in its Yellow Pages. Anyone using the number given for the Mexican Ministry of Tourism would have found themselves connected to a telephone sex service. The company said that only a few people had complained.

Birth of the day: Rita Hayworth (1918).

Death of the day: Frédéric Chopin (1849).

18 October

Good day for: *hedgehogs*
Bad day for: *the terminally ill*
Lucky profession: *chopstick salesman*

Major events of this day include the following:

1826: this year saw the last state lottery in Britain until 1994.
1867: the USA bought Alaska from Russia for $7.2 million.
1927: dancing bears were banned from the streets of Berlin.
1977: Hilary Bradshaw of Maidenhead became the first woman to referee a rugby match—between Bracknell and High Wycombe.
1982: on the A117 near Ludlow, Shropshire, Major Adrian Coles opened the first cattle grid with an escape-ramp for hedgehogs.
1987: the USA sold 18 million pairs of chopsticks to Japan.
1995: after a series of bank raids in broad daylight by a group known as the AIDS gang, the constitutional court in Italy amended a law that had prevented the imprisonment of terminally ill people. From this date on, judges could use their discretion.

Last words of the day: 'Die, my dear doctor? That's the last thing I'll do'—Lord Palmerston in 1865.

19 October

Good day for: *getting married in the nude*
Bad day for: *moustaches*
Lucky vehicle: *airship*

On this day in 1901, Alberto de Santos of Brazil flew around the Eiffel Tower in an airship in an attempt to capture the Deutsch Prize, worth about £1,000. He completed the trip in the permitted 30 minutes, but was 30 seconds too slow in climbing out of the gondola. After initially denying him the prize, the judges bowed to public pressure and awarded it to him anyway.

In 1970, this was the day that BP announced they had struck oil in the North Sea.

Self-sacrifice of the day: in 1995 Steve Marshall, a warehouse supervisor in Tewkesbury, Gloucestershire, agreed to trim his bushy moustache so that a new employee who was deaf could read his lips.

Wedding of the day: in 1997, Hsu Shao-tan, a stripper and former parliamentary candidate, married Wu Jung-chang in Taiwan's first nude wedding.

20 October

Affliction of the day: *halitosis*
Lucky number: *49*
Unlucky name: *Karolos Papoulias*

This was the day in 1818 when the 49th parallel was established as the boundary between Canada and the United States.

On this day in 1995, an Albanian was refused permission to change his name to Karolos Papoulias. It was not unusual for Muslim Albanians to adopt Orthodox Greek names in the hope of enhancing their work prospects, but the name he chose was that of the Greek Foreign Minister.

In 1997, the University of British Columbia announced a bad-breath testing service including both scientific analysis for halitosis and assessment by a human nose.

Prize of the day: in 1995 Rita, the ex-wife of American economist Robert Lucas, received half of her ex-husband's $1 million award for winning the Nobel Prize for Economics. There was a clause in their 1989 divorce settlement guaranteeing her half his winnings if he won a Nobel Prize before 31 October 1995.

21 October

Feast day of St Hilarion

Good day for: *fishermen*
Lucky substance: *cement*
Word of the day: *'tank'*

St Hilarion was one of the most popular hermits of the fourth century. He lived in a mud hut in Palestine, eating only figs, bread, oil and vegetables, and was held responsible for many miracles. As his fame spread, he was besieged with visitors, so fled to Egypt.

This was the day in 1824 when Portland cement was patented by Joseph Aspdin of Wakefield, Yorkshire. It was also the date of birth, in 1868, of Sir Ernest Dunlop Swinton, the man who gave us the word 'tank' to describe an armoured vehicle.

On 21 October 1995, Bertil Engzell was given a 200,000-kronor reward for a Smith and Wesson revolver he had fished from a river in Stockholm—the gun proved to be vital evidence in a racist killing.

On this day in 1915, women were allowed to become bus and tram conductors in London.

22 October

Good day for: *moving house*
Bad day for: *joking*
Terrifying day for: *dogs with vertigo*

On 22 October 1797 over Paris, André-Jacques Garnerin's dog became the first living creature to make a successful parachute jump from a hot-air balloon.

On this day in 1996, at the National Funeral Directors' Convention in Cincinnati, the Heirloom Pendant Collection launched a new range of pendants designed to let people wear their loved ones' ashes round their necks. It came in three designs: Teardrop, Infinity and Love.

In 1997, the 2,750-ton Gem Theatre in Chicago became the largest building ever moved on wheels as it was trundled to its new site.

Quote of the day: 'We don't lack a sense of humour, but Mr Pugh made this remark with a deadpan expression. The safety of our passengers is paramount'—a spokesman for Air 2000 explaining why Owen Pugh, 80, had been banned from a holiday flight from Newcastle-upon-Tyne to Cyprus in 1995. When asked if he had packed any electrical items, Mr Pugh had said: 'No, just the Semtex.'

23 October

Good day for: *lesbians*
Bad day for: *mobile phones*
Beware of: *falling dogs*

According to James Ussher, who became bishop of Meath in 1621, this was the date of the Creation in 4004 BC. John Lightfoot, vice-chancellor of Cambridge University, later pointed out that it happened at 9 a.m.

Douglas Jardine, captain of the English cricket team in 1932–3, was born on this day in 1900, and in 1915 W. G. Grace died.

Disaster of the day: in Buenos Aires in 1988 a dog fell from a 13th-floor window, landed on a 75-year-old woman and killed her. A bus driver swerved to avoid the ensuing commotion, killing a woman in the crowd, and a man watching it all died of a heart attack.

On 23 October 1996, a lesbian policewoman in Stockholm was the first to be given paternity leave as her partner gave birth to a baby conceived by artificial insemination. On the same day, mobile phones were banned from the state parliament of Andalusia.

Quote of the day: 'He loved playing cricket and gardening and had a pet pig called Violet'—Sara Karloff in 1995, on her father Boris.

24 October

Your unlucky name: *Fleur de Marie*
Your unlucky animal: *a pony*
Your unlucky composer: *Bizet*

A 13-year legal battle was finally lost on 24 October 1996, when the European Court of Human Rights voted 7–2 against the parents of a girl called Fleur de Marie Guillot, ruling that a French court's earlier refusal to allow them to register the name 'Fleur de Marie' did not violate the girl's rights with respect to privacy of personal and family life. The court had insisted she be legally called Fleur-Marie.

This was the day in 1857 when Cambridge University old boys in Sheffield formed the first football club. Exactly four years later, the Pony Express mail service from St Joseph, Missouri, to Sacramento, California, ceased operations after only 18 months in business.

Musical anniversaries: in 1915, the birth of the great Italian baritone Tito Gobbi; in 1930, of 'the Big Bopper' (John P. Richardson); in 1936, Bill Wyman of the Rolling Stones.

Quote of the day: 'As a work of art it is naught'—a review of Bizet's *Carmen* in the New York *Times* on 24 October 1878.

25 October

Feast day of St Crispin and St Crispinian, patron saints of cobblers

Good day to: *catch a train*
Hero of the day: *N. N. Dodds*
Recommended profession: *milliner or glove salesman*

'This day is called the feast of Crispian,' said Shakespeare's King Henry V before the Battle of Agincourt in 1415. Tradition has it that Crispin and Crispinian were brothers, possibly from third-century Rome, who preached the gospel and mended shoes in France.

More usefully, *Bradshaw's Railway Guide*, the world's first train time-table, was published upon St Crispin's Day in 1839. Another valuable publication today was Britain's first nuclear civil defence manual in 1957, which recommended, in the event of a nuclear attack, wearing hats and gloves and using lots of soap and water.

In the British general election on this day in 1951, Dartford was won by N. N. Dodds (40,094 votes), ahead of Margaret Roberts (27,760). The loser later attained fame under the name of Thatcher.

Quote of the day: 'C'est magnifique, mais ce n'est pas la guerre'— General Bosquet at the Charge of the Light Brigade this day in 1854.

26 October

Good day for: *a gunfight*
Lucky colour: *red*
Lucky profession: *crane driver*

Marriage features prominently in today's news: in 1909 a tax on bachelors was proposed in Austria, and in 1995 the first World Congress of Housewives was held in Buenos Aires.

Although this was the birthday, in 1685, of Domenico Scarlatti, the musical event of the day undoubtedly came in 1996 when Daniel Barenboim conducted a dance of 19 cranes on the Potsdamerplatz in Berlin, swaying back and forth to a tape of Beethoven's Ninth Symphony to celebrate the completion of a building project.

This was the day in 1881 when Wyatt Earp defeated the Clanton gang at the gunfight at the OK Corral. Today in 1929 it was announced that all London buses would be red, as yellow and green had proved to be unpopular in trials.

The first Madrid Marijuana Cup competition, held on this day in 1997, was inconclusive as the judges proclaimed themselves in no condition to declare a winner after sampling the entries.

27 October

Lucky profession: *getaway driver*
Satisfactory day for: *breasts*
Beware of: *soft-drink trolleys and Colombian kidnappers*

In Paris in 1901 on this day, a getaway car was first used in a shop robbery. The dangers of shopping were also highlighted in 1997 when six people were taken to hospital in Singapore after being hit by a runaway trolley of soft drinks in a hypermarket.

On 27 October 1997, a survey revealed that 71 per cent of American men were happy with the size of their partners' breasts and 57 per cent of American women were happy with the size of their own breasts. The same percentage of women, however, would rather go shopping on someone else's credit card than have sex.

On this day in 1662 Charles II sold Dunkirk to Louis XIV; and in 1996, the Colombian *El Tiempo* newspaper revealed that 45 per cent of the world's kidnappings take place in Colombia.

Record of the day: in 1996 Rowdy Blackwell, 15, set a new world record by playing 256 tambourines in 20.47 seconds.

Birth of the day: John Cleese (1939).

28 October

Good day for: *the blind*
Bad day for: *unsuccessful investors*
Good day for: *a quick haircut*

In 1996 on this day, Steve MacDonald, 24, became the first blind man to paddle a canoe round the British mainland. One year later, a judge in Perugia dismissed fraud charges against a registered blind man who had been found to have a driving licence. The man said that he had been cured of his blindness by visiting Lourdes on 13 December, feast day of St Lucia, patron saint of the blind.

On 28 October 1997 a new society was founded in Singapore to combat sexual ignorance, and in Israel, Dr Alexander Oshanyesky reported high levels of impotence on days associated with great stress, such as a stock market crash or the launch of Scud missiles.

In 1943, the Court of Appeal in London ruled that money a housewife saves from the housekeeping belongs to her husband.

Record of the day: in 1996 Trevor Mitchell of Southampton performed 18 haircuts in 60 minutes. The rules specified that each hair must be shortened by at least 2 centimetres – and no skinheads.

29 October

Good day for: *gays*
Bad day for: *transvestites*
Devotional act of the day: *e-mailing God*

The Israeli Internet company Virtual Jerusalem announced on 29 October 1996 that it was receiving between 15 and 20 prayers by e-mail each day, which it printed out and placed on the Wailing Wall.

In 1995 on this day, a man named Mohsen was beaten up by women commuters in Iran when he rode on a bus while dressed in women's clothing in order to win a bet with his father. He was later also sentenced to 20 lashes.

In 1996, gay prisoners at the Central Penitentiary in Tegucigalpa, Honduras, were encouraged to 'marry' other inmates to prevent the spread of AIDS. The marriages would be valid only within the prison, because gay marriages were illegal in Honduras.

On 29 October 1927, the Russian archaeologist Peter Kozlov discovered the tomb of Genghis Khan, and in 1986 the final section of the M25 orbital ring-road round London was completed.

Birth of the day: Paul Joseph Goebbels (1897), Nazi propaganda chief.

30 October

Good day for: *slim pets*
Lucky religion: *Islam*
Lucky ailment: *a headache*

Admiral 'Old Grog' Vernon died on this day in 1757. He earned his nickname through his order to ship's captains to dilute sailors' rum rations in order to reduce drunkenness.

This has been a good day for innovation: in 1905 Aspirin went on sale in Britain for the first time, and in 1997 a Belgian company introduced its 'Mikat' Islamic clock which can calculate prayer times and summon worshippers to prayer wherever they are in the world. On the same day, Petkin Pet Care Systems of Marina del Rey, California, introduced the PetTrim slimming pill for cats and dogs.

It was the day in 1938 when Orson Welles' notorious radio production of H. G. Wells' *The War of the Worlds* caused panic in the streets of America and one death through heart failure as listeners thought the Martians had invaded.

At a mass wedding in Seoul in 1988, the Reverend Sun Myung Moon joined together 6,516 couples. Most had met for the first time the day before.

31 October

....

Lucky mode of transport: *bicycle*
Lucky number: *5,145*
Lucky animal: *zebra*

Records of the day: in 1995 Helmut Kohl became Germany's longest-serving post-war Chancellor on this day, when he overtook Konrad Adenauer's 5,144 days; in 1997, a team of doctors in the Latvian capital of Riga claimed a world record for having sewn back four severed hands in five days—three had been cut off when their owners had been chopping trees down, and the fourth had fallen victim to a dough machine.

This was the day in 1888 when the first pneumatic bicycle tyres were patented by John Boyd Dunlop. In 1951 on this day, the first zebra crossings in Britain came into operation.

On 31 October 1995, William Warren, a prison inmate in Oklahoma, sued the authorities for the right to wear his own choice of undergarments. He said he needed to wear women's nylon knickers for medical reasons—being forced to wear white cotton was a 'cruel and unusual punishment'.

Births of the day: John Keats (1795), Dick Francis (1920).

1 November

....

Good day for: *openings*
Bad day for: *Batman*
Beware of: *earthquakes*

In 1848 on this day, W. H. Smith opened their first railway station bookstall; in 1946 *A Matter of Life and Death*, starring David Niven, opened in London at the Empire Cinema, Leicester Square, the first film to be given a Royal Command Performance; in 1959 the first stretch of Britain's first motorway, the M1, opened; and in 1982 Britain's fourth television station, Channel 4, began its transmissions.

This was also the date in 1922 when the first radio licences went on sale in Britain (costing ten shillings), in 1927 when the betting tax was first levied, and in 1956 when the first Premium Bonds went on sale.

Death of the day: Robin the Boy Wonder, killed by the Joker in 1988, following a phone-in poll in which readers of *Batman* comics voted for his death by 5,343 to 5,271.

Disaster of the day: the Lisbon earthquake of 1755, which destroyed the city and left an estimated 60,000 dead.

2 November

Bad day to: *frighten horses*
Picturesque day for: *rogues*
Vocation of the day: *US president*

Two US presidents were born on this day: James Polk (1795) and Warren Harding (1865). Other great Americans to have this birthday were the frontiersman Daniel Boone (1734) and actor Burt Lancaster (1913).

Crime-fighting in Britain took a step forward on 2 November 1871 with the first photographs of criminals and the inauguration of the 'rogues' gallery'. In 1896 the first motor insurance policies were issued, excluding coverage for damage caused by frightened horses.

Invention of the day: the unsinkable lifeboat, patented in 1785 by Lionel Lukin, a London coach-builder.

Puzzle of the day: in 1924 the *Sunday Express* published the first crossword in a British newspaper. This, incidentally, happened on the 21st anniversary of the first publication of the *Daily Mirror*.

Deaths of the day: George Bernard Shaw (1950) and James Thurber (1961).

3 November

Historic day for: *space dogs*
Furious day for: *a woman scorned*
Hero of the day: *Lord Nelson*

This was the day in 1957 when Laika, a stray picked off the streets of Moscow, became the first dog in space. It did not survive its trip aboard Sputnik II, but in 1997 the 40th anniversary of its death was marked by the unveiling of a plaque at the Institute of Aviation Medicine in Moscow.

Another notable event of 3 November 1997 was the appearance in court in Canberra of Jacqueline Martin, 39, charged with pouring a bucket of manure over a bride at a wedding. She had intended to throw it over the groom, her ex-fiancé, but could not get close enough. She attended the wedding disguised in moustache and beard.

On 3 November 1843, the statue of Horatio Nelson began to be hauled to the top of its column in Trafalgar Square.

Deaths of the day: M. Popov of Bulgaria, the first pilot killed in warfare, in 1912; and sharpshooter Annie Oakley (Phoebe Anne Oakley Moses) in 1926.

4 November

....

Good day for: *shopkeepers*
Bad day for: *treason*
Unfashionable item of the day: *the monocle*

Remember, remember the 4th of November—for this was the day when Guy Fawkes was arrested for attempting to blow up the Houses of Parliament. But it was late at night, and news of it only spread on the 5th, which thus became the night of Guy Fawkes celebrations.

In 1879 on this day James Ritty, a saloon-owner in Ohio, patented the cash register, and in 1914 the first fashion show was held at the Ritz Carlton Hotel in New York. This was also the day in 1996 when Tetley Bitter redesigned their traditional label, changing the image of the old huntsman portrayed on it to a more modern version without a monocle. According to a spokesman, it had made him look old-fashioned.

Crime of the day: in 1995, a man in China was arrested for selling the corpse of a young woman to a peasant couple as a bride for their dead son. The price was about £40.

---

5 November

....

Lucky day for: *fat crooks*
Dumb day for: *Germans*
Dish of the day: *Christmas pudding*

In 1917 on this day, the War Office agreed to supply Christmas puddings to British troops in France. Ten years later, Britain's first automatic traffic lights came into operation in Wolverhampton.

In 1932, out of respect for the nearby football team, London Transport agreed to change the name of Gillespie Road Underground station to 'Arsenal'.

In Wellington, New Zealand, on 5 November 1997 William Dickie, 43, was sentenced to 12 months' house arrest because he was too big for prison clothing or a prison bed. Mr Dickie weighed 305 kilograms. On the same day, a survey showed that 90 per cent of Germans think their fellow countrymen are growing less intelligent.

Births of the day include actresses Vivien Leigh (1913), Elke Sommer (1940) and Tatum O'Neal (1963), as well as two halves of notable singing duos: Ike (of Ike and Tina) Turner (1931) and Art (of Simon and Garfunkel) Garfunkel (1942).

---

6 November

Good day for: *dwarfs*
Bad day for: *vampires*
Recommended profession: *saxophonist*

This was the day in 1893 when Dracula died in Bram Stoker's novel. A less fictional death on the very same day was that of the composer Tchaikovsky, victim of a cholera epidemic in St Petersburg.

It's a good day for inventions: in 1814 Adolpho Sax was born, inventor of the saxophone, and in 1928 Jacob Schick patented his 'shaving implement', the world's first electric razor.

Research result of the day: in 1995 scientists in North Dakota reported the result of an experiment showing that dwarf mice that had been denied a particular growth hormone lived up to twice as long as normal mice kept in identical conditions.

6 November 1995 was also the day when some Swaziland MPs called for new laws to protect men and boys from being raped by women. They argued that the present law on rape was discriminatory and all laws should protect both sexes equally.

7 November

Good day for: *disappearing*
Lucky profession: *Greek postman*
Unlucky number: *99*

On this day in 1996 Richard Rosenthal of Cambridge, Massachusetts, was convicted of beating his wife to death and impaling her heart and lungs on a stake after she complained that he had burnt their dinner.

Scientific advance of the day: in 1908, Ernest Rutherford announced the detection of a single atom.

Award of the day: in 1995, the *Bookseller* magazine gave its Odd Title of the Year award to *Greek Rural Postmen and Their Cancellation Codes*.

Disappearance of the day: Lord Lucan, in 1974.

Quote of the day: 'A few years back we had a guy who had swallowed 90. This is a record'—police superintendent Eugene Opperman, after waiting for a drug courier who had swallowed 99 condoms full of cocaine to produce the evidence in the lavatories of a South African airport on 7 November 1995.

8 November

Good day for: *senior civil servants*
Bad day for: *cubists*
Disastrous day for: *frogs*

This was the day in 1970 when the Great Bengal Frog War began, which left thousands of frogs dead after a frantic love-in in Sungaisiup, Malaysia.

Other disasters: on 8 November 1913 cubism was banned at the Salon d'Automne art exhibition in Paris, and in 1987 a Californian sentenced to 17 years for murder attempted to sue a juror for falling asleep during his trial.

On this day in 1995, fines for drunken walking were announced in Colombia. In 1995 also, researchers at University College, London, found that senior civil servants live longer than junior ones, and a judge in Italy ruled that blaspheming against the Virgin Mary is not a crime.

Quote of the day: 'It is important to have comfortable feet'—Francis Thomas, Britain's most successful exam-taker, in 1995, explaining how warm slippers contributed to his success in passing 70 O-levels, 16 A-levels and 1 S-level, and in getting an Open University degree.

9 November

Good day for: *childbirth*
Bad day for: *political leaders*
Popular day for: *abolition*

Wilhelmina Carstairs was born in Edinburgh on this day in 1847, when her mother was given chloroform in the first use of anaesthetics in childbirth. Another notable birth, on this day in 1841, was that of Albert Edward, first son of Queen Victoria, who later became Edward VII. He was the last person to be born first in line to the British throne. In 1799 on this day, Napoleon Bonaparte became First Consul of France and in 1960 John F. Kennedy was elected President of the USA.

This is a remarkable day for deaths, including British prime ministers Ramsay MacDonald (1937) and Neville Chamberlain (1940), and Presidents Chaim Weizmann (1952) of Israel and Charles de Gaulle (1970) of France.

This was also the day in 1888 when Jack the Ripper claimed his final victim, Marie Kelly.

Flogging was abolished in the British army on 9 November 1859, and the abolition of capital punishment in Britain came into force on 9 November 1965.

10 November

....

Recommended form of transport: *motor-cycle*
Adventurous day for: *sperm*
Beware of: *stampeding elephants*

Paul Daimler became the world's first motor-cyclist on this day in 1885 when he rode his father Gottlieb's new invention for six miles. The most exciting journey of the day, however, was the 4-kilometre trip across Paris taken in 1994 by 300,000 sperm samples from the Centre for the Study and Conservation of Human Eggs and Sperm—the first move of a sperm bank in Europe.

Over 30 people were treated for injuries when four elephants ran amok during the Lord Mayor's Show in London on this day in 1930.

Innovations of the day: in 1995, Hsu You-shend and Gary Harriman were partners in the first (not legally binding) gay wedding in Taiwan, and in 1997 Britain celebrated its first National Curry Day.

Tim Rice, who wrote the musical *Chess*, was born on this day in 1944, and Garry Kasparov became world chess champion on 10 November 1985.

Quote of the day: 'Dr Livingstone, I presume', uttered by Henry Morton Stanley at Ujiji on Lake Tanganyika in 1871.

11 November

Feast day of St Menas, patron saint of sheep caravans

....

Good day for: *staggering*
Hopeful day for: *the woolly mammoth*
Lucky day for: *vegetarians*

All early representations of St Menas, an Egyptian martyr who died early in the fourth century, feature him accompanied by two camels. Nobody knows why, but he is said to be good at finding lost sheep.

On 11 November 1995, the Japanese biologist Kazufumi Goto said that he believed it will be possible to fertilise an Indian elephant with the frozen sperm of a woolly mammoth. He announced plans to mount an expedition to find a suitable donor.

On this day in 1947, the British government announced that vegetarians would be granted extra potato rations, and in 1952 John Mullin and Wayne Johnson demonstrated the first video recorder.

Birthdays: Fyodor Dostoevsky (1821), Kurt Vonnegut (1922).

Quote of the day: in 1996, the Scottish Council on Alcohol described a 2 per cent rise in counselling sessions for people with drink problems as a 'staggering increase'.

12 November

Good day to: *go fishing*
Bad day to: *show off to your girlfriend*
Daring day for: *a young man on a flying trapeze*

Jules Léotard gave his first performance on this day in 1859, without a safety net, as the original daring young man on the flying trapeze at the Cirque Napoléon in Paris. The tight-fitting garment he wore was later named after him.

Another who risked his life on this day was Kevin Hill, 18, of Connecticut, who was treated in hospital in 1995 after shooting himself in the genitals when he tried to show his girlfriend the sawn-off shotgun tucked into his trousers. After being treated for a cut and powder burns, he was charged with illegal discharge of a firearm.

Death of the day: the much maligned Canute, King of England, Denmark and Norway, who died in 1035.

Catch of the day: in 1974 a salmon was caught in the River Thames, the first since the 1840s.

Gas of the day: argon, first isolated by Lord Rayleigh, who was born on this day in 1842.

13 November

Bad day for: *spelling*
Unlucky profession: *rainmaker*
Lucky number: *888*

Festo Kazarwa, a rainmaker in Kabale, Uganda, was beaten to death by villagers on this day in 1988, after crops and homes were destroyed by hailstones. He had earlier threatened to summon up hail if the villagers did not show him more respect.

The brassière was patented by Mary Phelps Jacob on this day in 1914, and in 1987 the BBC transmitted its first commercial for condoms.

Two notable events happened on 13 November 1995: in China, two 23-year-old girls, Qian Linping and Ni Junfang, completed a new world record by living in a room for 12 days with 888 snakes of which 666 were cobras; and in Israel the family of Yitzhak Rabin complained about his name being misspelt on a square newly renamed in his honour.

This day in 1896 was the last that British law required a man with a red flag to walk in front of a car. A wise move, since the speed limit was about to be raised from 4 mph to 14 mph.

14 November

Bad day for: *mistresses*
Lucky football club: *Arsenal*
Unlucky number: *4*

Nell Gwyn, mistress of Charles II, died on this day in 1687, and Louise de Keroualle, mistress of Charles II and Duchess of Plymouth, died in 1734.

Birth of the day: John Curwen (1816), Congregationalist minister and inventor of the tonic sol-fa scale.

On 14 November 1849, *The Times* published a letter from Charles Dickens in which he pronounced himself 'astounded and appalled by the wickedness' of a public execution.

In 1934, England's soccer team against Italy included seven Arsenal players, and in 1995 the Taiwanese government announced that it would allow residents to omit the number 4 from house addresses because the word for 'four' sounds like 'death'.

In 1963 on this day, a volcanic eruption created the island of Surtsey off Iceland, and in 1969 colour television transmissions began in England.

15 November

Good day for: *lost knickers*
Exciting day for: *fresh peas*
Mixed day for: *the deaf*

One king and one queen retired on this day: King Pedro II of Brazil abdicated in 1889, leaving his country a republic, and in 1968 the largest passenger ship ever built, the *Queen Elizabeth*, completed her final voyage.

The good news for the deaf is that in 1901 on this day, Miller Reese of New York patented a hearing-aid. The bad news is that it was not portable.

On this day in 1969, Birds Eye frozen peas were the subject of the first colour television advertisement in Britain, and in 1995 in South Korea Lee Jee-yung, 23, became the first woman to bungee-jump from a flying paraglider.

Survey of the day: research by Radio Rentals in 1996 revealed that the average British sofa had £2.50-worth of assets stuffed beneath or behind its upholstery. The study also claimed that 24 per cent of London sofas include a pair of knickers among their concealed items.

16 November

Auspicious day for: *musicals*
Hopeful day for: *unmarried pets*
Unlucky profession: *highwayman*

In Gerona, Spain, on this day in 1997 the country's first match-making agency for pets opened, keeping on record photographs of its clients and a description of the qualities sought in a mate.

The Sound of Music opened on Broadway on this day in 1959, on the anniversary of the day that Oklahoma—the only state to give its name to a musical—became the 46th state of the Union in 1907. More musically than either of these, however, this was the day in 1848 when Chopin gave his final public performance in a charity concert at the Guildhall in London.

Death of the day: Jack Sheppard, highwayman, hanged at Tyburn in 1724 after escaping execution on four earlier occasions.

Quote of the day: 'The majority of women in the country no longer cover their heads, and this is one strong reason why there has been little rain'—Msweli Mdluli, member of parliament in Swaziland, speaking about his country's drought on 16 November 1995.

17 November

Expensive day for: *dinner*
Heroic day for: *a duck*
Revealing day for: *women*

In 1869 on this day, the first bicycle road race was held between Paris and Rouen and was won by James Moore of England, and in 1883 the first experimental relay race (not on bicycles) was held at Berkeley, California.

In 1944, a quacking duck alerted the city of Freiburg, Germany, to an imminent air raid. A statue was later erected in its honour.

This is a day of mixed accomplishments for women: in 1880, London University for the first time awarded a BA degree to a woman, and in 1970 the first page three girl appeared in the *Sun* newspaper.

On 17 November 1997 three businessmen, celebrating a deal and a birthday, spent a record £13,091 on dinner at Le Gavroche restaurant in London. The wine bill alone amounted to £12,870. On the very same day the Californian Supreme Court ruled that feet are not deadly weapons, as defined by the law of aggravated assault.

18 November

Recommended breakfast: *porridge*
Confusing day for: *timekeepers*
Unlucky name: *Mortimer*

This was the 'day of two noons' in the United States in 1883, when clock times were synchronised throughout the country following the National Railway Time Convention. At an agreed moment, all town-hall clocks, previously registering local time, were changed to a standard American noon. In Britain in 1996, however, this was National Porridge Day.

Mickey Mouse made his first appearance on this day in 1928, though an identical character had previously appeared under the name 'Mortimer Mouse'.

Innovation of the day: in 1963, push-button phones were introduced by the Bell Telephone Corporation.

Book of the day: on 18 November 1477, Caxton published *The Dictes and Sayengis of the Philosophres* by Earl Rivers, the first dated book to be published in England.

Notable birth: George Gallup, father of the opinion poll, in 1901.

19 November

Innovative day for: *contraception*
Good day for: *vegetarianism*
Lucky colour: *white*

In 1995, this was National Dunking Day in Britain. Research into the event revealed that only 36 per cent of Britons were brave enough to dip biscuits into drinks in public.

On 19 November 1959 the Archbishop of Canterbury, Geoffrey Fisher, said that adultery should be a criminal offence. In 1996 a Swedish entrepreneur, Hans Backman, announced his invention of the tie-on condom, secured by two elasticated bands, to ease the problems experienced by fumblers. But on this day in 1997 Elcio Berti, the mayor of Bocaiúva, Brazil, banned the sale of contraceptives in an attempt to increase the size of the town and maintain levels of government funding that were dependent on population numbers.

On this day in 1996, Orange County Transit Authority paid $50,000 to settle a suit brought by a vegetarian driver who had been sacked for refusing to distribute hamburger coupons to his passengers.

In 1951, it was the day that the white football was officially sanctioned.

20 November

Good day for: *hyphens*
Bad day for: *spies*
Lucky book: War and Peace

This was the day in 1906 when Charles Stewart Rolls and Frederick Henry Royce hyphenated their surnames so as to make cars together.

In 1944, the people of London knew that the end of the war was in sight when the lights came on in Piccadilly Circus after five years of blackout. Exactly one year later, the Nuremberg War Crimes trial opened.

In 1979 it was the day that Anthony Blunt, Surveyor of the Queen's Pictures, homosexual and spy, was stripped of his knighthood.

Birthdays: Robert Kennedy (1925), Count Leo Tolstoy (1828).

Death of the day: General Franco (1975).

Artistic events of the day: the first performance of Beethoven's *Fidelio* in 1805; Salvador Dali's first one-man show, in 1929.

Wedding of the day: Lt Philip Mountbatten married Princess Elizabeth in Westminster Abbey in 1947.

21 November

Beware of: *the demon drink*
Meal of the day: *dog*
Unlucky day for: *transsexuals*

This was the birthday in 1888 of Adolph Marx, who became Arthur Marx when Hitler brought his first name into disrepute, and then became better known as Harpo Marx when he took up the harp and stopped talking.

The most notable death of the day was that of an unnamed man who was killed in 1906 when 200,000 gallons of hot whisky burst from vats in a Glasgow distillery.

On 21 November 1995, the Court of Appeal in South Korea ruled that dog-meat is edible food.

On 21 November 1996, the Court of Appeal in London ruled that a transsexual, whose 17-year marriage to an heiress had been declared null and void when she discovered her husband was a woman, was not entitled to a share of the marital home and wealth. The ruling was based on the conclusion that he had committed a 'profound betrayal of trust'.

22 November

Feast day of St Cecilia, patron saint of music

Recommended goal: *Wimbledon championship*
Lucky number: *22 (or possibly 66)*
Lucky writing implement: *ball-point pen*

Nobody is quite sure whether St Cecilia ever existed, but according to a sixth-century tale she was a Christian girl who, on her wedding day, told her pagan husband that she had consecrated her virginity to God and persuaded him to honour the deal and be baptised himself. The story tells of her singing to God 'in her heart'—which was enough, apparently, for her to be made patron of music.

This is the birthday of two tennis champions: Billie-Jean King (née Moffatt) in 1943, and Boris Becker in 1967.

The North Korean leader Kim Jong Il held a special ceremony on 22 November 1996 to honour the 22 groups of triplets serving in his country's armed forces, which are believed to have more triplets than any other army in the world.

The first Biro went on sale on this day in 1946, invented by the Hungarian Laszlo Biro and made in England.

23 November

Unlucky profession: *fireman*
Winning numbers: *37 and 50*
Favourite TV programme: Dr Who

Three biscuit-factory workers from Glasgow won the world's first biscuit-dunking championships on this day in 1997, making their way through 37 soggy biscuits in a minute. Another great sporting achievement of the day was the 50th consecutive Sumo wrestling victory of grand champion Chiyonofuji, only the fifth man in history to achieve this feat.

Births of the day: William 'Billy the Kid' H. Bonney in 1859 and Boris Karloff in 1887.

23 November 1995 was also the birthday of the fire chief of Arlanda airport in Sweden. While he was waiting for the plane he had boarded to take him off on a celebration holiday, his colleagues decided to cheer him on his way in the most appropriate way they could think of—on their approach to the plane, two of the fire engines stopped in time, but the third crashed into the wing, causing £50,000-worth of damage.

On this day in 1889, the first juke-box was installed in San Francisco, and in 1963 the first episode of *Dr Who* was transmitted on BBC TV.

24 November

Your lucky name: *Christine Banks*
Your unlucky animal: *the crocodile*
Bad day to: *win a drama award*

Lee Harvey Oswald, assassin of President Kennedy, was himself shot dead by Dallas nightclub-owner Jack Ruby on this date in 1963—exactly 104 years after the publication, in 1859, of Darwin's *Origin of Species*. Freddie Mercury died on this day in 1991, while among the notable births, we must mention Henri de Toulouse-Lautrec (1864) and the cricketers Herbert Sutcliffe (1894) and Ian Botham (1955).

A survey of major winners on Littlewood's lotteries scratch-cards published on this day in 1997 revealed that the luckiest woman's name was Christine (or Tina) and the luckiest surname was Banks.

On 24 November 1996, Loughborough University announced plans to set up an anti-stress course for football managers, and on the same day crocodile meat went on sale in Sainsbury's.

Quote of the day: 'Oh fuck me, I'm last up and I'm desperate for a piss'—Michael Gambon, when it was announced at the *Evening Standard* Drama Awards in 1995 that he had won the Best Actor award.

25 November

Propitious moment for: *a first night*
Convenience food of the day: *evaporated milk*
Seasoning of the day: *garlic*

Birth of the day: Joe DiMaggio (1914), baseball star and husband of Marilyn Monroe.

Death of the day: Yukio Mishima (1970), Japan's most popular author, who ritually disembowelled himself after attacking Japan for its meekness in agreeing a constitution banning rearmament.

John Mayenberg of St Louis, Missouri, patented evaporated milk on this day in 1884. And in 1996 the government of Taiwan appealed to its people to eat more garlic—excess production had caused a catastrophic fall in prices.

On 25 November 1896 in London, William Marshall received the first summons for parking his car illegally, but the charge was later dismissed.

In 1952, the theatre world's longest-running production had its first night: Agatha Christie's *The Mousetrap* at the Ambassadors Theatre in London. On this day one year later, England suffered their first ever soccer defeat at Wembley, losing 6–3 to Hungary.

26 November

Dangerous profession: *tarot card reader*
Lucky way to give birth: *Caesarean section*
Unlucky body part: *lip*

The first twins ever to be delivered by Caesarean section were born on this day in Manchester in 1928. Another notable birth was that of Charles Schulz, creator of the *Peanuts* strip cartoon, in 1922—which was precisely the day that Howard Carter and the Earl of Carnarvon took their first peek into the tomb of Tutankhamun.

On 26 November 1996 in Monterrey, Mexico, a tarot card reader called Gloria Garza Villanueva, 40, was reported to be in a serious condition in hospital after having been shot twice in the head by a customer who had not liked the fortune she had predicted for him.

Meanwhile, on the same day in Zimbabwe, Lazarus Nzarayebani, a legislator for the town of Mutare, was fined 1,000 Zimbabwean dollars (about £60) for biting the lip off a political opponent in a brawl.

John Loudon McAdam, who gave his name to a method of surfacing roads, died on this day in 1836.

27 November

Good day for: *bad sex*
Even better day for: *sexual equality*
Fat day for: *Switzerland*

This was the day in 1893 when women in New Zealand voted for the first time in a national election anywhere in the world. Britain did its bit for sexual equality on the same day in 1914, when Miss Mary Allen and Miss E. F. Harburn became the first policewomen.

On 27 November 1996, the Bad Sex in Fiction awards were made in London. This winning book of the year was *The Big Kiss* by David Huggins, which edged out other contenders because its sex scenes were judged to be 'irrelevant to the plot'. Exactly one year later, a survey in Switzerland revealed that one in three of the population was 'overweight', 12 per cent were 'obese', and 4 per cent were 'grossly obese'.

Birthday: Anders Celsius (1701), inventor of the centigrade temperature scale.

Quote of the day: 'Non'—Charles de Gaulle, when Britain applied to join the Common Market in 1967.

28 November

Game of the day: *billiards*
Unlucky toy: *Barbie Doll*
Beware of: *sideburns*

This was the birthday in 1837 of John Wesley Hyatt, inventor of the composition billiard ball.

Political news of the day: in 1988, cabinet secretary Robert Armstrong admitted he had been 'economical with the truth' and in 1990 Margaret Thatcher delivered her resignation note to the queen.

On 28 November 1996, the actor Bruce Willis admitted that he uses Barbie Dolls for target practice, and on the same day the former Chilean dictator General Pinochet gave officers three pieces of advice: don't gossip about the military, watch your drink, and don't grow sideburns if you are visiting London.

Quote of the day: 'It is a pity to focus everything on the currency board when there are such beautiful breasts around'—Bulgarian actress Anya Pencheva, announcing in 1996 that she would display a plaster cast of her breasts in the National Theatre to help men take their minds off economic problems.

29 November

Good day to: *avoid going shopping*
Popular day for: *dwarfs*
Lucky day for: *false teeth*

In 1996 in Vancouver, this was declared Buy Nothing Day by several groups fed up with the commercialisation of Christmas.

It was a good day in 1995 for Cor Stoop, a 60-year-old Dutchman who had lost his false teeth in a bout of seasickness two months earlier: today he got them back from a fisherman who found them in a cod's stomach.

On 29 November 1996, a judge in Sardinia granted a temporary injunction stopping an 84-year-old pensioner from marrying his 19-year-old fiancée. The ruling was issued at the request of the man's children.

Quote of the day: 'I think it's clear there are relatively few people who are physically suitable for this work'—a spokesman for the actors' union Equity explaining the problems caused by 14 Christmas productions of *Snow White* in 1995 when 'we have only 37 persons of restricted growth on our register'.

30 November

Busy day for: *writers*
Goalless day for: *soccer*
Potentially divisive day for: *married Nazis*

This was the day in 1935 when non-belief in Nazi ideology became grounds for divorce in Germany.

John Bunyan was born on this day in 1628, Jonathan Swift followed him in 1667 and Mark Twain made it three in 1835.

The first international soccer match in 1872 ended in a 0–0 draw between England and Scotland. The fixture was hardly propitious, since it was played in Glasgow on St Andrew's Day and St Andrew is the patron saint not of footballers but of golfers.

On 30 November 1995, a bugging device was found at the HQ of the Lothian and Borders police in Edinburgh. They decided it had probably been put there by a police employee who could not tell the difference between an ordinary plug adaptor and a listening device.

Quote of the day: 'One or the other of us has to go'–allegedly Oscar Wilde's last words, spoken to the wallpaper in a Paris Hotel on 30 November 1900.

---

1 December

Good day to: *change sex*
Bad day for: *elks*
Beware of: *lampreys*

On this day in 1996 Matthew Taylor, a lecturer in archaeology at the University of Bradford, announced that man has been obsessed with sex since the dawn of time. His conclusions were supported by a 5,000-year-old Siberian rock engraving of a Stone Age man on skis trying to penetrate an elk.

He might also have cited the evidence of 1 December 1952, when George Jorgenson, formerly of the US armed forces, became a woman in the first sex-change operation, or 1 December 1953, when Marilyn Monroe appeared as the first centre-spread in *Playboy*.

Henry I died on this day in 1135 after eating 'a surfeit of lampreys', and exactly 520 years later, in 1655, Samuel Pepys married Elizabeth St Michel.

1 December 1919 was the day Lady Astor took her seat as the first female member of parliament; and the same day in 1990 was when the two halves of the Channel Tunnel met in the middle.

---

2 December

....

Bad day for: *cut-throat razors*
Fatal day for: *John Brown's body*
Superfluous day for: *shirts*

On 2 December 1996, the *Liberation Daily* newspaper in China drew attention to the country's huge overproduction of shirts, which had left a shirt mountain amounting to three shirts for everyone in the country.

The Marquis de Sade, who gave his name to sadism, died on this day in 1814 in the lunatic asylum at Charenton. Another to share this death day was John Brown, the American anti-slavery campaigner who was hanged in 1859.

In 1697 on this day the newly rebuilt St Paul's Cathedral was opened, and in 1929 Britain's first public phone boxes came into operation.

In 1901 King Camp Gillette finally marketed the safety razor with a two-edged disposable blade, for which he had received a patent four years previously. And on 2 December 1982 the first artificial heart was fitted, to Barney Clark, in Utah. He survived for three more months.

3 December

....

Sporting day for: *rats*
Venomous day for: *snakes*
Bad day for: *the overweight*

In 1920 on this day, Rudyard Kipling was awarded £2 damages for the unauthorised use of his poem 'If' in a medical advertisement. In 1961, Matisse's painting *Le Bateau* was finally put the right way up at the Museum of Modern Art in New York, after it had hung upside-down for 46 days without anyone noticing.

On 3 December 1995, Finnish researchers demonstrated the success of their animal-conditioning experiments by arranging a basketball match between two teams of rats at the Finnish Science Centre in Helsinki. On the same day, a bill was filed in the Philippines parliament to exclude morticians from hospitals, especially near operating theatres and intensive care units, where they had been touting for business.

In 1996 a Swede was arrested for threatening to kill his neighbour with a poisonous pet snake, and on this day in 1997 an Egyptian woman was denied her plea for alimony on the grounds that she had forced her husband to leave her because she had let herself get fat.

4 December

Good day for: *beautiful men*
Recommended mode of travel: *train*
Unlucky profession: *exorcist*

On 4 December 1996, Brad Rogers became the first male finalist in the Miss Australia competition when he was voted 'Miss Victoria Fundraiser'.

This day in 1154 was the last time an Englishman was elected Pope: Nicholas Breakspear became Adrian IV. Another unusual election happened on 4 December 1995, when Nelson Mandela was awarded the title of 'Santa Claus of the Year' by the government of Greenland. Also in 1995, this was the day when Shanghai voted to ban fortune-telling and exorcism from its temples.

Other notable events of the day: in 1872, the *Marie Céleste* was found adrift and abandoned; in 1934 it was announced that all rail fares in the UK would be cut to a penny a mile; and in 1937 Desperate Dan made his first appearance in the *Dandy*.

Deaths today: John Gay, composer of the *Beggar's Opera*, in 1732; Benjamin Britten, composer of several other operas, in 1976.

5 December

Good day to: *make a phone call or post a letter*
Even better day to: *have a drink*
Prime suspect of the day: *a koala bear*

In 1839, this was the day when British postal charges ceased to be dependent on distance but became a uniform fourpence per half-ounce. In 1958 phone calls became simpler, with the STD system eliminating the need to make long-distance calls via an operator. The first STD call was from the Queen to the Lord Provost of Edinburgh.

It was the day in 1933 when prohibition came to an end, repealed by the 21st Amendment, and the day in 1996 when the Iranian parliament passed a bill banning the official use of all foreign words and phrases.

Quote of the day: 'Although it is extremely unlikely that koala prints would be found at the scene of a crime, police should at least be aware of the possibility'—Maciej Henneberg, a biological anthropologist and forensic scientist at Adelaide University, commenting, on 5 December 1996, on the discovery that koalas' fingerprints are almost identical to human ones.

6 December
National day of Finland

....

Health food of the day: *pizza and tomato ketchup*
Good day for: *merchants, thieves, sailors and travellers*
Bad day for: *pigs and bachelors*

This is the feast day of St Nicholas, patron saint of merchants, thieves, sailors, travellers, children, pawnbrokers and others, as well as the model on whom the legend of Santa Claus was built. The name comes from a Dutch dialect version, Sinte Klaas, for St Nicholas.

In 1557 on this day, a pig at the commune of Saint-Quentin, France, was sentenced to be 'buried all alive' for having devoured a little child, and in 1926 Mussolini imposed a tax on bachelors.

In 1995 the Isle of Wight Zoo announced that in view of the bad weather it would be giving special training to its Siberian tigers, because they had never seen snow before. On the same day, US researchers reported that pizza and tomato ketchup can provide protection against prostate cancer.

On this day in 1774, Austria became the first country to introduce a state education system.

---

7 December
....

Recommended profession: *boxing referee*
Unlucky appendage: *pigtails*
Lucky investment: *rubber*

On 7 December 1997, a poll among teenagers in the Russian far east revealed that 25 per cent of girls would like to become prostitutes and 27 per cent of boys wanted to become racketeers.

Two years earlier, industry sources in India reported soaring prices for rubber, caused by rapidly increasing worldwide demand for condoms.

Birth of the day: Noam Chomsky (1928), father of modern linguistics and vigorous anti-Vietnam protester.

Deaths of the day: Charles Brooks in Fort Worth Prison, Texas, in 1882, the first person to be executed by lethal injection; and William Bligh (1817), former captain of the *Bounty*.

This day in 1907 saw the first referee—Eugene Corrie—appear inside a boxing ring (at the Gunner Moir versus Tommy Burns fight in London), and it was on this day in 1911 that China outlawed the pigtail.

---

8 December

Feast day of St Budoc

....

Good day to: *fake an orgasm*
Popular day to: *be circumcised*
Immaculate day for: *the Virgin Mary*

The legend of St Budoc relates that his mother, Azenor, was thrown into the sea off Brest in a cask in which she gave birth to Budoc. Five months later, so the story goes, they were washed up, in good health, in Ireland.

On this day in 1996, a survey revealed that almost 70 per cent of unmarried Colombian women and 40 per cent of married ones fake orgasms. Exactly one year later, Malaysia's Minister of Culture, Arts and Tourism predicted that mass circumcision ceremonies could become a tourist attraction.

On 8 December 1854 a papal bull was issued by Pius IX declaring that the Virgin Mary was preserved from all sin from the moment of her birth. In 1934 the London–Australia airmail service was inaugurated and in 1981 Arthur Scargill was elected president of the National Union of Mineworkers.

9 December

....

Good day for: *a public execution*
Drink of the day: *draught beer*
Favourite television soap: Coronation Street

Births of the day: John Milton (1608), and Clarence Birdseye (1886), frozen food pioneer, who got the idea from watching Inuit pack their food in ice when he worked in the fur trade in Alaska.

Deaths of the day: Sir Anthony Van Dyck (1641), Flemish painter knighted by Charles I; and Joseph Bramah (1814), inventor of the beer pump.

This was the day in 1967 when Nicolae Ceausescu became president of Romania, and in 1990 when Lech Wałeşa became president of Poland.

It was the day in 1783 when Newgate Prison in London held its first public executions, and the day in 1960 of the first episode of the long-running soap opera *Coronation Street*. Douglas Fairbanks Jr and Kirk Douglas never appeared in *Coronation Street*, though they were both born today, in 1909 and 1916.

10 December

Good day to: *go topless*
Bad day to: *let your children stay up late*
Beware of: *the dog*

When the first McDonald's opened in Belarus on this day in 1996, police with truncheons beat off the large crowd besieging the building, most of whom thought—wrongly—that free food was being offered. On the very same day a Spanish hunter, Antonio Iglesias, was wounded in his bottom while hunting wild boar when his dog inadvertently stepped on the trigger of his shotgun.

Other events of 10 December 1996: in Ontario, the Court of Appeal ruled that a woman may go topless as long as the act is not considered sexual—indecency, it was considered, is not possible without a sexual connotation. Meanwhile, in Plano, Texas, a woman was sentenced to 90 days' probation for failing to get her five-year-old son to bed early (he had repeatedly been late for his kindergarten classes).

Event of the day: 'A Grand Exhibition of the Effects Produced by Inhaling Nitrous Oxide, Exhilarating or Laughing Gas' at Union Hall, Connecticut, on 10 December 1844.

11 December

Feast day of St Daniel the Stylite

Recommended window covering: *venetian blinds*
Bad day for: *handkerchiefs*
Optimistic day for: *men*

Daniel the Stylite (from the Greek word for 'pillar') lived on a platform between two pillars. He was a disciple of St Simeon the Stylite, who lived on a pillar. Daniel only came down from his platform once in 33 years. He lived to the age of 84 and was buried at the foot of one of the pillars.

On 11 December 1995, a poll in Britain revealed that 20 per cent of men hope for sex after the office Christmas party but that only 1 per cent of women think it likely; in 1997 on this day, another survey found something on which men and women agree: they both said that handkerchiefs were what they would least like to receive as a Christmas present.

Venetian blinds were patented on this day in 1769, by a Londoner called Edward Bevan. And on this day in 1996 fans of Gillingham football club were warned that they risked a life ban if they brought celery into the ground.

12 December

Letter of the day: *S*
Recommended way to travel: *by hovercraft*
Unlucky profession: *tax collector*

On 12 December 1901 the first transatlantic wireless signal, the letter S, was sent from Poldhu in Cornwall to Signal Hill, St John's, Newfoundland. And in 1988, satellite pictures were first transmitted to British betting shops to let people see the races live.

In 1955 on this day Christopher Cockerell patented the hovercraft, and in 1995 irate businessmen broke the nose of one tax collector, fractured the leg of another and chased several more for a kilometre down the street in Modinagar, India.

On 12 December 1996, scientists at Stanford University published their discovery that a single gene controls the entire sex life, from choice of mate to love-making ritual, of the male fruitfly.

Quote of the day: 'Every character in headlines is as large as a washbasin and even characters in the text are as large as bowls'—Xinhua news agency report in 1995 on the attempt by the Xian *Evening News* to create as a special edition the largest newspaper in the world.

13 December

Controversial day for: *Santa Claus*
Good day to: *weigh yourself*
Nice day for: *an ice-cream*

On this day in 1995, the Canadians gave Santa Claus his very own post code (H0H 0H0) and the Americans arrested him. The trouble came in the District of Columbia where Salvatore, 45, in red cloak and white beard, was leading some carol-singers. After someone complained about the noise, he was arrested for disorderly conduct, but a counter-charge of molesting a Santa Claus was laid against the police.

Other notable events of the day: in 1779 the Smithfield Cattle and Sheep Society had their first show in London; in 1878, Holborn Viaduct was illuminated with the first electric street lighting in Britain; in 1884, the coin-operated weighing machine was patented by Percy Everitt; in 1903, ice-cream cones were patented by Italo Marcione of New York; in 1937 Sellotape was first marketed in Britain; and in 1989, the first concert using sign language was given by a deaf choir from South Wales at Gwyn Town Hall in West Glamorgan.

14 December

Unlucky pet: *seal*
Beware of: *dead geese*
Democratic day for: *women over 30*

Two Roman journalists were fined for letting a seal swim in the Trevi fountain on this day in 1951. According to the law, only coins may be thrown in.

Anne Osinga, the chairwoman of the Friesian Society for the Protection of Birds, was taken to hospital with concussion and a broken cheekbone on 14 December 1995 after she had been knocked down by a dead goose—the bird had been shot by one of her companions.

This was the day in 1918 when women over 30 voted for the first time in a British general election. In 1954 it was the day divorce was legalised in Argentina, and in 1973 it was when Idi Amin of Uganda started a 'Save Britain' fund to help Britain out of its economic crisis.

Sporting event of the day: the first ever tie in a cricket test match, Australia v. the West Indies at Woolloongabba in 1960.

15 December

Lucky tree: *maple*
Lucky game: *'Trivial Pursuit'*
Unlucky species: Rattus norvegicus

In 1654 on this day, the meteorological office in Tuscany became the first to record daily temperatures, and exactly 325 years later, on 15 December 1979, Chris Haney and Scott Abbott invented 'Trivial Pursuit'.

In 1996, *Eva* magazine published a survey of what women would most like to have if they could be granted just one wish. The most popular response was world peace (42 per cent), but 14 per cent would rather have the housework magically done for them, 10 per cent wanted never to grow old, and 1 per cent wanted a different husband.

On 15 December 1997, a doctor in New York was convicted of trying to extort $5 million from McDonald's by planting a fried rat's tail in a burger. The tail was found to have come from *Rattus norvegicus*, the breed found in laboratories such as the one the doctor worked in.

In 1939 on this day, nylon was first produced commercially in Seaford, Delaware, and in 1964 Canada adopted the maple leaf as its flag.

16 December

Feast day of St Adelaide, Holy Roman empress

Lucky name: *Buddy*
Unlucky name: *John*
Good day to be: *beautiful and good*

St Adelaide was the widow of King Lothair of Italy, but was imprisoned by his successor, Berengar II, then rescued by Otto the Great of Germany, whom she married in 951. St Odilo, abbot of Cluny, described her as 'a marvel of beauty and goodness'.

After intense public speculation, Bill Clinton finally announced on this day in 1997 that he was going to call his new pet dog 'Buddy', 'after my beloved uncle who died earlier this year'.

Divorce of the day: the 13-year marriage between Napoleon Bonaparte and Josephine de Beauharnais was dissolved on this day in 1809.

Quote of the day: 'I don't like your game 'Big John' because my name is John, and it is an insult to call me a toilet'—letter of complaint from nine-year-old John Slovacek of Lafayette, California, to Parker Bros in 1995, complaining about their game 'Big John' in which players throw green 'scuzzies' into a lavatory.

17 December

Hat of the day: *bowler*
Gastronomic treat of the day: *dog food*
Composer of the day: *Beethoven*

On this date in 1997, a poll revealed that 39 per cent of American voters thought Santa Claus would be a democrat, 22 per cent thought he would register as a Republican, 23 per cent were not sure, and 13 per cent called him an independent. Charles Dickens' *A Christmas Carol* was published on this day in 1843.

In 1995, this was the day Asda supermarkets announced their first Christmas dinner for dogs. Supreme Chunks Christmas Dinner was made with turkey, stuffing, chipolatas, carrots, peas, potatoes and gravy.

Escaping from the Christmas theme—this was the day in 1849 when William Coke paid 12 shillings for the first bowler hat, which was made by Thomas Bowler for Lock and Co. of St James's.

On 17 December 1885, Jem Smith beat Jack Davies in the last official bare-knuckle British heavyweight championship fight.

In 1770, Ludwig van Beethoven was born.

18 December

Hairstyle of the day: *crew cut*
Hallucinogenic day for: *reindeer*
Bad day for: *violins*

This was the day in 1737 when the great violin-maker Antonio Stradivari died. His technique has never been equalled, but the secret was probably in his recipe for the varnish.

On this day in 1863 slavery was abolished in the United States, and in 1970 divorce was legalised in Italy. In 1996, a tribunal in Australia ruled that military crew cuts for men were not sexually discriminatory in a case brought by an air force fitter who wanted to wear his hair long.

Santa Claus and his reindeer came under academic scrutiny on this day in 1996, when Dr Patrick Harding of Sheffield University put forward the theory that they originated with a magic-mushroom hallucination cult. He pointed out that witch-doctors in Lapland took fly algaric before treating patients, and that reindeer also ate it—the only animals to consumer hallucinogenic narcotics by choice.

Birth of the day: actress Betty Grable (1916) and film director Steven Spielberg (1947).

19 December

Floor covering of the day: *linoleum*
Lucky shoes: *blue suede*
Significant day for: *Soviet leaders*

Leonid Brezhnev was born on this day in 1906, and his 74th birthday, in 1980, was the day of the death of Alexei Kosygin, with whom he had once shared power in the USSR.

Invention of the day: linoleum, patented by Frederick Walton of London in 1863.

Musical event of the day: in 1955, Carl Perkins recorded 'Blue Suede Shoes'.

Medical discovery of the day: according to a paper in the *British Medical Journal* in 1996 smoking can turn your hair grey, and it also appears to be associated with baldness in men.

Scientific discovery: this was the day in 1996 when a group of Cambridge University scientists led by Charles Ellington finally solved the problem of how bees and moths fly. Using a mechanical model of a giant hawkmoth, they were able to demonstrate the existence of vortices capable of lifting the bulk of the body.

20 December

Good day for: *video-recorders*
Bad day for: *trams*
Lucky fish: *coelacanth*

An investigation of cheating in exams in Egypt reported on this day in 1996 that many students had gained admission to universities by pretending to be blind. Of the 90 students enrolled under special schemes for the blind, 25 were found to be fakes.

Also on 20 December 1996, a poll revealed what invention had been found by Americans to make life easier for them. The most popular response was the video-recorder, followed by computers and mobile phones.

This was the day in 1952 when the second coelacanth was caught—the fish had been thought to have been extinct for some 50 million years until one was caught in 1938 off South Africa. Many other fish had to be caught for the opening, on this day in 1928, of Harry Ramsden's fish and chip restaurant in Bradford, which grew to become the most famous in the world.

Other events of the day: in 1957 Elvis Presley was called up to join the army; in 1996, the last trams ran in Vienna.

21 December

Good day for: *rich widows and spinsters*
Game of the day: *basketball*
Lucky day to: *have your leg amputated*

The Isle of Man decided on this day in 1840 to give votes to women—as long as they were widows or spinsters and owned property with a ratable value of £4 a year or more. Six years later, on 21 December 1846, Robert Liston used ether as a general anaesthetic for the first time while performing a leg amputation at University College Hospital in London.

On this day in 1891, in the gymnasium of the YMCA at Springfield, Massachusetts, James Naismith invented the game of basketball. Another innovatory recreation first appeared on this day in 1913 when the *New York World* published the first crossword.

If you were born on this day, you stand a higher than average chance of becoming a national leader: it was the birthday of British prime minister Benjamin Disraeli in 1804, of Russian leader Joseph Stalin in 1879, and of Austrian statesman Kurt Waldheim in 1918. It was Jane Fonda's birthday, too, in 1937.

22 December

Element of the day: *oxygen*
Disputatious profession: *chicken-sexer*
Beware of: *open manholes*

On 22 December 1877, Raoul Pictet of Geneva produced liquid oxygen for the first time. Another first followed in 1922, when the London police sanctioned trials of covered-top buses.

This has generally been a day of problems: in 1943, the British government said there were only enough turkeys in the country to provide a Christmas dinner for one family in ten; in 1987, thieves in China stole 2,249 manhole covers and demanded a ransom for their return; and in 1997 in Australia a row broke out at a poultry farm over the hiring of South Korean chicken-sexers. The farm management claimed that the Koreans were more accurate and quicker than Australian chicken-sexers, but the Australians said it was only a trick to get them to work for lower wages.

Birth of the day: opera composer Giacomo Puccini (1858).

Deaths of the day: writers George Eliot, pen-name of Mary Ann Evans (1880) and Beatrix Potter (1943).

---

23 December

Lucky profession: *taxi-driver*
Lucrative profession: *hair-straightener*
Good day for: *Santa Claus*

This was the day in 1987 when Santa Claus met the Pope, after delicate negotiations between the Vatican and the Finnish Tourist Board. Earlier notable events of the day were Joseph Hansom patenting the 'safety cab' in 1834; Sarah Breedlove, a hair-straightener, becoming America's first self-made millionairess; and Van Gogh cutting off his ear in 1888.

The earliest recorded sighting of the word 'cheeseburger' was on 23 December 1941, when it was seen over a shop in Burbank, California. Exactly six years later, the transistor was invented.

Births of the day: Russian tsar Alexander I (1777) and German Chancellor Helmut Schmidt (1918).

Deaths of the day: St Philip of Moscow (1569) and King Leopold II of Belgium (1909).

Quote of the day: 'These are the times that try men's souls'—a line penned by Thomas Paine, author of *The Rights of Man*, on 23 December 1776.

24 December

Good day for: *listening to the radio*
Bad day for: *the Beatles*
Watch out for: *German bombs*

This day has many musical connotations. It was the day in 1920 of Enrico Caruso's last concert, and in 1974 of the legal dissolution of the Beatles partnership. More positively, Christmas Eve saw the first performance of the carol 'Silent Night' at a church in Bavaria in 1828, and the first performance of Verdi's *Aida* at the opening of the Suez Canal in 1871.

On 24 December 1908 the world's first aviation show was held in Paris, and in 1922 the first play commissioned for radio was broadcast by the BBC. Written by Phyllis M. Twigg, it was called *The Truth about Father Christmas*.

In 1508 on this day London houses first received piped water, and 24 December 1914 was the first time that a German bomb landed on Britain.

Births of the day: world chess champion Emanuel Lasker (1868) and actress Ava Gardner (1922).

Death of the day: explorer Vasco da Gama (1524).

25 December

Good day for: *family rows*
Bad day for: *kissing in the street*
Unhappy Christmas for: *Romanian dictators*

In 1913, a New York couple were arrested and fined $15 for kissing in the street on Christmas Day. A couple in Oakland, California, had an even worse Christmas in 1983 when the 70-year-old wife shot and killed her 72-year-old husband because he was having an affair.

This is a good day for coming to the throne: William the Conqueror was crowned on Christmas Day in 1066, and Emperor Hirohito acceded to the throne of Japan on Christmas Day 1926. A less fortunate leader was Nicolae Ceausescu of Romania who was executed, together with his wife Elena, on Christmas Day 1989.

The painter Maurice Utrillo was born on this day in 1883, and exactly a hundred years later the surrealist painter Joan Miró died.

The first recorded 25 December Christmas celebration was in Rome in 336, and the first recorded Christmas tree in Britain was put up by Queen Charlotte on Christmas Day in 1800.

26 December

The Feast of Stephen

Good day for: *looking out*
Bad day for: *English usage*
Art form of the day: *pantomime*

The Stephen on whose feast Good King Wenceslas supposedly looked out when the snow lay deep and crisp and even was the first Christian martyr, who was stoned to death in AD 35 or 36.

The first Christmas pantomime, *Harlequin Executed*, was performed at Lincoln's Inn Fields Theatre in London on this day in 1717. Appropriately enough, it was on Boxing Day too, in 1908, that Jack Johnson became the first black world heavyweight champion by defeating Tommy Burns in Sydney, Australia.

This was the day in 1898 when Marie and Pierre Curie, engaging in some post-Christmas experimentation, discovered radium.

Births of the day: Charles Babbage (1792), mathematician and inventor of a calculating machine; Mao Zedong (1893), father of modern China.

Deaths of the day: President Harry S. Truman (1972), Nobel Prize-winning playwright Samuel Beckett (1989), and lexicographer Henry Watson Fowler (1933), author of *A Dictionary of Modern English Usage*.

27 December

Day of Nine Evils in Bhutan

Good day for: *evolution*
Equal day for: *women*
Pet of the day: *cat*

The first performance of James Barrie's play *Peter Pan* took place on this day in 1904. The role of Captain Hook was taken by actor-manager Sir Gerald du Maurier, father of the novelist Daphne du Maurier.

In 1871, the world's first cat show took place on 27 December at the Crystal Palace in London. The animal best associated with this date, however, is the *Beagle*, the ship on which Darwin set out on his voyage of discovery in 1831.

This was the day in 1975 when the Sex Discrimination and Equal Pay Acts came into force in Britain.

Births of the day: Louis Pasteur (1822), chemist and bacteriologist; Marlene Dietrich (born Maria Magdalene von Losch in 1901), actress and singer; Gérard Depardieu (1948), actor.

Quote of the day: 'Silly and inconsequential'—H. E. Krehbiel's description of Puccini's *La Bohème* in his review in 1900.

28 December

Good day for: *dry-cleaning*
Confectionery of the day: *chewing-gum*
Sport of the day: *women's cricket*

This was the day of the Tay railway bridge disaster in Scotland in 1879 when a bridge collapsed as a train passed over it. As William McGonagall wrote in 'The Tay Bridge Disaster':

> Beautiful Railway Bridge of the Silv'ry Tay!
> Alas, I am very sorry to say
> That ninety lives have been taken away
> On the last Sabbath day of 1879
> Which will be remember'd for a very long time.

Other events of the day: M. Jolly-Bellin discovered dry-cleaning by accident when he spilt oil and turpentine on his clothes in 1849; William Fenley Semple patented chewing-gum in 1869; an earthquake in Messina, Sicily, killed around 80,000 in 1908; the first women's test match, England against Australia, was played in 1934.

Birth of the day: President Woodrow Wilson (1856).

Death of the day: his widow, Edith Bolling Wilson (1961).

29 December

Unlucky body part: *knee*
Unlucky garment: *trousers*
Good day for: *inventors named Charles*

One British prime minister was born and one died on this day: William Ewart Gladstone was born in 1809 and Harold Macmillan died in 1986. Further notable births include Jeanne Antoinette, the Marquise de Pompadour (1721), mistress of Louis XV; Charles Macintosh (1766), inventor of the raincoat that bears his name; Charles Goodyear (1800), inventor of vulcanised rubber.

On 29 December 1852, Emma Snodgrass was arrested in Boston for the crime of wearing trousers. Exactly one hundred years later, the first transistorised hearing-aid went on sale.

On this day in 1890, the Battle of Wounded Knee took place in South Dakota, the last major battle between US troops and the Red Indians. The following year, on the same day, radio took a big step forward when Edison patented the 'transmission of signals electrically'. This was also the day in 1914 when the first zeppelin was spotted off the Bristol coast.

30 December

....

Drink of the day: *Coca-Cola*
Garment of the day: *bloomers*
Good day for: *Elvis Presley*

This was the date of birth in 1851 of Asa Griggs Candler, the man responsible for developing the formula for Coca-Cola; and it was the date of the death, in 1894, of Amelia Jenks Bloomer, a liberated lady who designed her own ankle-length undergarments. Richard Rodgers, composer of musicals, also died this day in 1979.

Firsts of the day include the first public concert in London in 1672 and the first coffee to be planted in Hawaii in 1817.

On 30 December 1994, a rare earth tremor in Britain threw residents of Manchester and Darlington from their beds.

In 1809 on this day, the city of Boston banned the wearing of masks at balls.

In 1947, King Michael of Romania gave up his throne.

In 1996, US District Judge Vanessa Gilmore ruled that a bar in Houston could continue calling itself 'Velvet Elvis' without being a threat to the image of Elvis Presley.

---

31 December

Feed Yourself Day in Benin

....

Bad day for: *looking out of the window*
Unreliable day for: *New Year's resolutions*
Game of the day: *'Monopoly'*

This was the day in 1696 when the window tax was imposed in Britain. Despite its unpopularity, it was not abolished until 1851. A more useful innovation of the day was Dr R. N. Harger's 'drunkometer', a primitive breathalyser, which was first used on the streets of Indianapolis on this day in 1938.

Perhaps the most successful invention of the day was the game of 'Monopoly', patented on New Year's Eve 1935 by Charles Darrow.

The least successful invention of the day appears to have been J. D. Schneiter's 'rocket mail', which he patented in France on 31 December 1870 but which has still not be taken up by the French postal authorities.

Finally, a survey published on 31 December 1997 showed that 46 per cent of New Year's resolutions are broken within a week and 17 per cent will not even last a day.